KWB8

STRIP QUILTING PROJECTS 3

Projects from the "Strip Quilting 3" series
as shown on PBS-TV Stations

by

Kaye Wood

ISBN No: 0-944588-13-1

Kaye Wood Publishing Co. 4949 Rau Road West Branch, Michigan 48661 517-345-3028

A SPECIAL THANK YOU
TO THE SPONSORS
OF MY
THIRD TELEVISION SERIES
"STRIP QUILTING 3"

VIKING SEWING MACHINE CO.
11750 Berea Road
Cleveland, OH 44111
Manufacturers of
VIKING SEWING MACHINES and HUSKYLOCK SERGERS

and

HOBB'S BONDED FIBERS
P.O. Box 151
Groesbeck, TX 76642
Manufacturers of
POLY-DOWN batting, fiberfill, THERMORE & Pillow Inserts

AND THANK YOU TO:

Concord Fabrics for most of the fabric used
and to
Marty Lawrence of Flint, MI for her segment on hand-dyeing fabrics
Information on her hand-dyed fabrics is available
by sending a legal size self-addressed envelope:
Marty Lawrence
P.O. Box 4602
Flint, MI 48504

PHOTOGRAPHY BY: JUDY JOHANNES PHOTOGRAPHY
and WILLIAM E. WOOD

Television series "Strip Quilting" produced by:
David Larson Productions
P.O. Box 26497
Milwaukee, WI 53226

TABLE OF CONTENTS

CHAPTER 1: INTRODUCTION

CHAPTER 2: PROJECTS

CHAPTER 3: PLANNING & FINISHING YOUR QUILT

SEMINARS & WORKSHOPS
by

KAYE WOOD
4949 Rau Road
West Branch, MI 48661
517-345-3028

NEW TECHNIQUES for
FAST, EASY and ACCURATE MACHINE STRIP PIECING--
ALL WITHOUT TEMPLATES
developed by Kaye Wood

SEMINARS (Lecture /Demonstration /Trunk Show)

*3 different 2-hour seminars -- a total of 6 hours
*quick tips and ideas for machine patchwork
*over 150 step-by-step samples & finished quilts
*good for large or small groups
*informative and entertaining

1. CREATIVE PATCHWORK
   Fast methods for traditional patchwork
   Combining and creating new patterns
   Ideas taken from several of Kaye's books

2. LOG CABIN VARIATIONS
   Fast strip piecing of the basic Log Cabin
   Reversible quilts
   Triangles & diamonds

3. STARMAKERS
   New & easier ways to make stars,
   Tumbling blocks, Spiderwebs & Diamonds

SIT-AND-SEW WORKSHOPS

*Several different 6-hour workshops
*Limited to 30 students -- sewing machines needed
*Learn Kaye's techniques for accurate piecing

1. LOG CABIN DIAMONDS
2. LOG CABIN TRIANGLES
3. REVERSIBLE QUILTS
4. BASIC LOG CABIN
5. STRING STAR VARIATIONS--Jane's Morning Star
6. SMALL LONE STAR
7. BISCUIT or PUFF QUILTS

CHAPTER 1:

INTRODUCTION

to
"STRIP QUILTING PROJECTS, Volume 3"

These projects are all included in my third television series, "STRIP QUILTING 3".

Strip piecing and accurate angles --
that makes the STRIP LIKE A PRO Program special and unique.

STRIP PIECING is
cutting strips
sewing them into combination strips
cutting them into cut combinations --squares, rectangles, triangles, diamonds, wedges
sewing them into hundreds of designs.

The STRIP LIKE A PRO Program is made up of all of my books, tools, and videos.

BOOKS---go step-by-step through the techniques for easy and accurate strip piecing.
STARMAKER TOOLS--- insure accurate angles.
VIDEOS--- visualize the steps for more accurate piecing and to show you a wide range of color & design possibilities.

When you combine STRIP PIECING with the STARMAKER tools,
you insure accurate angles:

STARMAKER 5---
18 degree angle for 20-piece Dresden Plates & 5-piece fans
72 degree angle for 5-pointed stars, diamonds & wedges

STARMAKER 6---
60 degree angle for 6-pointed stars, diamonds, triangles & wedges

STARMAKER 8---
22-1/2 degree angle for 16-piece Dresden Plates & 4-piece fans
45 degree angle for 8-pointed stars, diamonds & wedges
90 degree angle for square, rectangles & wedge triangles

SUPPLIES NEEDED

The supplies which will make your STRIP PIECING PROJECTS easier and more accurate are:

The Starmaker 5 tool
The Starmaker 6 tool
The Starmaker 8 tool
A heavy plastic ruler
The Olfa rotary cutter & mat
Iron
Magnetic seam guide
Double-faced basting tape
The View-A-Strip
The View-A-Square

ACCURACY -- CUTTING, SEWING, PRESSING

TYPES OF FABRIC TO USE IN YOUR QUILT:

100% cotton is the easiest fabric to sew and quilt. It will eliminate a lot of problems. Cotton is the best choice when you plan to hand quilt. However, if you plan to machine piece and quilt, other fabrics can usually be incorporated into your quilted items. If you plan to wash your quilt, all the fabrics should be able to be washed in the same way. I do occasionally mix cottons and blends--except when the design calls for pieces to be cut on the true bias, e.g., the Lone Star, because cottons and blends stretch differently on the bias.

FABRIC PREPARATION

Fabric for quilts should be washed and dryed before using. Just before washing, I cut the four corners off my fabric. This reduces ravelling, but most of all, it tells me my fabric has been washed and dryed when I take it off the shelf. Washing & drying fabric removes the sizing, reduces the possibility of shrinkage and dyes that run.

MEASURING

Always use the same ruler to cut the width of your strips within any one project. Rulers are not always the same; and changing from one ruler to another can result in strips that are not cut the same width. By using the same ruler, your measurements will be more accurate.

WORKING WITH THE DESIGN OF THE FABRIC:

To center a particular design in a square, use the View-A-Square, which is adjustable. You can view fabric as it will look when cut from squares from 1" to 5". It will also let you view rectangles of different sizes. This is particularly helpful when you want to cut blocks from large floral patterns or unusual fabrics.

CUTTING THE STRIPS

All of the designs in this book are made with strips of fabric. Most strips are cut across the width of the fabric (44"/45"), from selvedge edge to selvedge edge.

Fabrics with a lengthwise design can be more effective when the strips are cut lengthwise. Fabrics such as stripes, or the poly-cotton moires I like to use, will give you a completely different look depending on whether they are cut across the width or lengthwise. Use the VIEW-A-STRIP tool to help you decide which way will be more effective.

To cut strips with the rotary cutter:

Fold the fabric in half with selvedge edges together.

Lay the folded fabric on the rotary cutter mat. (Be sure the fabric lays flat, even if the cut or torn edges are not together.) The fold of the fabric should be lined up with one edge of the mat or a grid line on the mat. Cut the fabric perpendicular to the fold to straighten one edge, using the rotary cutter and a heavy plastic ruler. Fold the fabric once more by bring the folded edge to the selvedge edge--the fabric will now be in 4 layers; the shorter length will be easier to cut. Cut the rest of the strips needed. Use the lines on the ruler to cut accurate strips, e.g., to cut 1 1/2" wide strips, place the 1 1/2" line on the ruler at the cut edge of the fabric. Pull the rotary cutter along the edge of the ruler.

SEWING ACCURATELY

Sewing accurately is very important. You might want to try a magnetic seam guide on your machine to help you line up the strips of fabric as you sew. It really does make a difference. But the magnetic seam guide can cause problems with the computer in other brands of computer sewing machines; so check with the manufacturer of your machine. It causes no problems with my Viking.

Usually in patchwork 1/4" seam allowances are used. With the techniques in my books, any seam allowance will work, but you must be consistent.

Chain Stitch- stitching from one piece of fabric directly on to the next without cutting thread. In strip piecing, cut combinations are usually sewn to long strips of fabric; then the long strips are cut. Cut combinations are also sewn to other cut combinations one right after the other.

Stay Stitch-a row of stitching through just one layer of fabric. It helps to stabilize the edges of combination strips and makes it easier to turn on a fold line.

Top Stitch-stitching done through all layers of fabric. A top stitch can be straight stitch or decorative.

Combination Strips -- two or more strips of fabric sewn together lengthwise.

Cut Combinations -- pieces cut from the combination strip. They can be squares, rectangles, triangles or diamonds.

Serging Machine or Serger- sews, overcasts and trims the seam allowance all at the same time. Most of the projects in this book can be done on either the sewing machine or serger. Serging patchwork is faster and can be just as accurate. Pressing seam allowances is faster and easier because the seams are already overcast together. Your patchwork will also have neater and flatter seam allowances.

MATCHING SEAMLINES

There are several methods which I use to match seamlines:

Double-faced basting tape--for matching points. The tape with its paper or plastic backing is placed within the seam allowance on the right side of the fabric. Press in place with your fingers. Remove the paper backing. Lay the second piece of fabric, right sides together, on top of the taped fabric. Check on the right sides to make sure the seam lines or points match perfectly. Then finger press the two layers of fabric together. Sew on the seam line. Remove the basting tape. Press the seam allowances.

Pinning. Pinning is usually done with the grain line, which is usually along the seamline. This is especially important when pinning angled cuts.

The pins should follow one seamline or the other when pinning diamonds and stars together.

There are color photos in the center of the book with step-by-step directions for matching and pinning diamond strips together.

Finger Pinning - holding seam allowances together with fingers as they start to feed through the sewing machine.

If the seam allowances go in opposite directions, try to sew them together with the top seam allowance laying toward the needle and away from you. The feed dogs on your machine will push the top layer of fabric into the seam on the bottom fabric. This is the easiest seam line to match.

If the top seam allowance lays away from the needle and toward you, you will have to hold the seam lines together firmly as you sew toward them.

PRESSING ACCURATELY

Pressing correctly is important in all kinds of patchwork; it becomes even more important when you work with angles in your designs.

Seam allowances are usually pressed to one side in patchwork; BUT before pressing the seam allowances toward one side, press the seamline in the position it was sewn. This will help to keep the stitches locked in the center of the fabric. It will also restore any stretching that occurs when sewing bias cut fabric.

Accurate pressing is insured by:

1. pressing with the grain of the fabric.
2. pressing from the right side of the fabric.
3. no steam

Pressing with the grain. Pressing (an up and down motion with the iron) is much different than ironing (a side to side gliding motion). Ironing can stretch fabric if it goes along the crosswise grain of the fabric, e.g., moving the iron along the length of the **strip.**

Pressing from the right side of the fabric --Pressing from the wrong side can result in pleats forming at the seamline. To press from the right side of the fabric, follow these directions:

1. Each time a new strip is added, lay the patchwork on the ironing board; the new strip will be wrong side up, the rest of the quilt block will be right side up.
2. Use the side of the iron to press the new strip away from the finished piece. The seam allowance will lay toward the new strip.

No Steam -- Steam is useful in clothing construction to put shaping into the pieces of a garment. Using steam in strip piecing can cause the strips of fabric to stretch.

CHAPTER I

PROJECT 1: MACHINE QUILTING

Before doing any machine quilting, you need to prepare your machine.

1. Clean your machine. Oil it, if it is not self-lubricaitng.
2. Change your needle. Use a size 80 or 12.
3. Set your stitch length to 10-12 or 2.5 cm.
4. Use a regular straight stitch foot or zigzag foot with a flat bottom.
5. For channel or straight line quilting, try a quilting guide on your machine.
6. Use a good brand-name thread.
   (A poor quality thread can cause problems with your machine)
7. For quilting in the ditch, use a good invisible (clear or smoke) thread in your needle; bobbin thread should match the quilt backing.

Step 1: Cut several 12" sample squares of fabric and different weights of batting.
Layer and safety pin baste 3 pieces together
(top, batting, backing).

Step 2: Draw a line in the center of the sample square.
If you don't have a quilting guide, draw lines 1" apart on the sample.
If you have a guide, use the guide to space your quilting lines.

Bring bobbin thread through to the top of the quilt. Hold both bobbin and top thread. Start quilting by either dropping feed dogs and taking several stitches or shorten the stitch length to lock your stitches.

When turning corners, lock stitches to prevent a thread from pulling across the corner.

Don't pull or push the quilt through the machine but let the feed mechanism of the machine feed the quilt through.

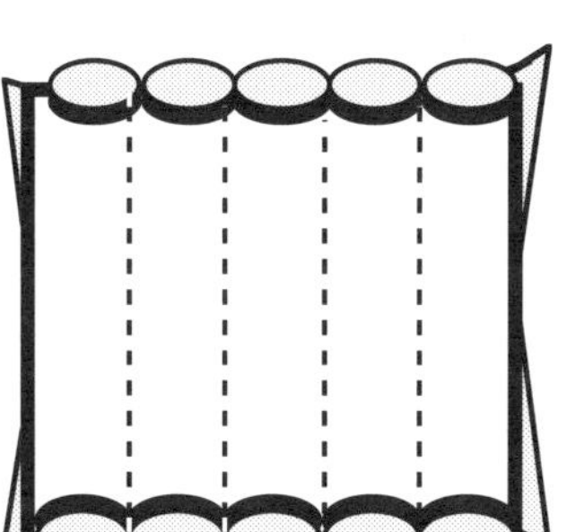

Machine quilt a row of stitching in the middle of the sqaure.

Make any machine adjustments necessary:

<u>pressure foot</u> - if the top layer of fabric is fed through the machine faster than the backing fabric, loosen the pressure on your presser foot.
<u>stitch length</u> - depending on the weight, or loft, of the batting, you may want a longer stitch length.
<u>presser foot</u> - you may want to experiment with different flat-bottomed feet to see which works the best. If none of your feet give you a nice quilting stitch, you may want to invest in a walking or even-feed foot.

Step 3: Adjust the quilting guide so your stitching lines will be 1" apart.
The quilting guide rides right along your previous stitching line as you stitch a new line. It helps to keep an even distance between stitching lines.

Stitch another quilting line and make more adjustments if necessary.

Continue sewing quilting lines 1" apart.

After you have found the right combination of pressure, stitch length, presser foot and thread, try some of these quilting lines on your samples.

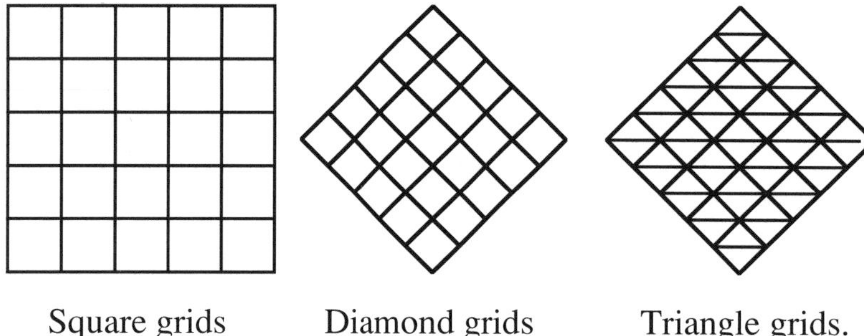

Square grids Diamond grids Triangle grids.

Also try quilting with

1. Double needle
2. Triple needle
3. Narrowest zigzag stitch

And try stitching with a basting zigzag (long wide stitch) with invisible thread over ribbon, soutache braid, cording, yarn.

Be sure to try all different weights of batting, fleece and Thermore.

FREE MOTION QUILTING

Free motion quilting requires some practice. The fabric moving mechanism is not used--so you must do all of the fabric moving.

It is also called meander stitching because it allows you to meander all over the quilt, and even do intricate curved lines, without turning the fabric.

1. Replace the presser foot on your machine with a darning foot.
2. Lower the feed dogs (in the darning position) or set the stitch length at 0.
3. Bring the bobbin thread up through the fabric.
4. Hold the bobbin and needle thread.
5. Start stitching with needle down in the fabric.

The darning foot will put pressure on the fabric at the exact time the stitch is forming.

If you are doing free-motion quilting in just a small area, you might want to use a machine embroidery hoop for added control.

PROJECT 2: CHRISTMAS STOCKING
(A quilt-as-you-go project)

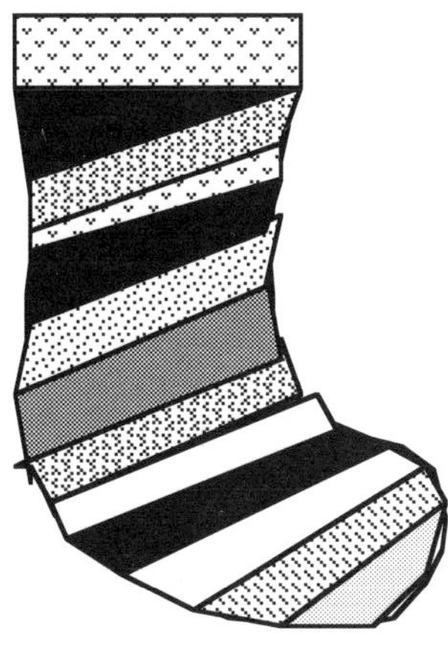

Fabric:

Strips of assorted widths for strip piecing.
2 pieces of fleece or Thermore cut in stocking shape
2 pieces of backing cut in stocking shape
Top band - 3" x 8"
Binding & hang tab 2" x 20"

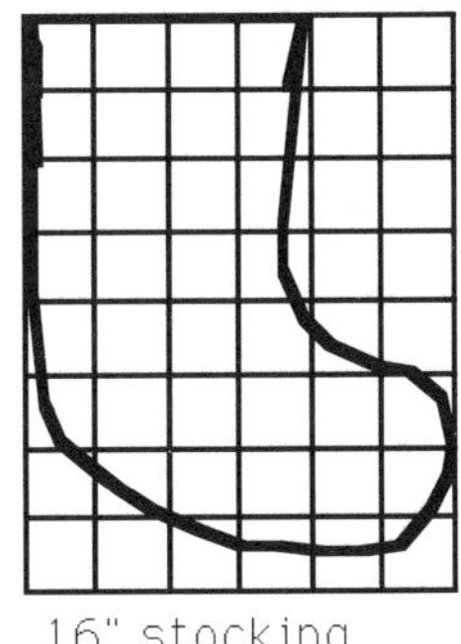

Step 1: Make a pattern for the stocking.

(7" x 16")

Cut 2 backing pieces and 2 fleece using the pattern.
Cut 1 band for the top of the stocking

Step 2: Baste zigzag (long, wide stitch) together 1piece of fleece and 1 stocking back.
Mark the band line 3" down from the top of the fleece.

Step 3: Sew two strips, right sides together, to the fleece and backing.
Open up the strip on top.
Pin in place.

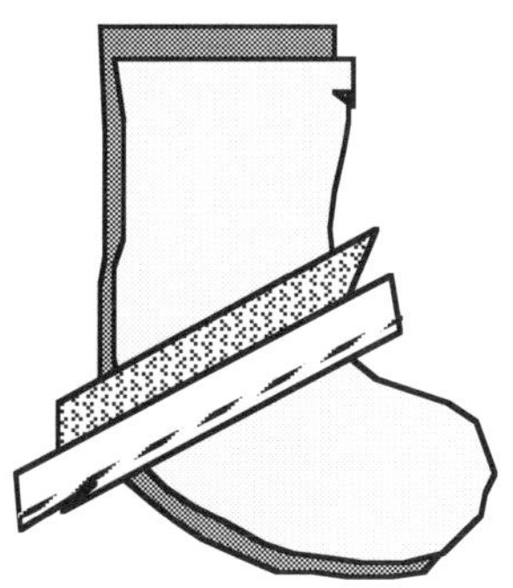

Step 3: Sew a third strip, right side down, on top of one of the other strips.
Open the strip up. Pin.
Continue adding strips, right sides together, until the stocking is covered.

Step 4: Sew the band, right sides together, at the band line 3" from the top of the stripped stocking.
Be sure to completely cover the raw edge of the top strip.
Baste zigzag together the edges of the band and the top of the stocking back and fleece.
Use a decorative stitch or machine embroidery a name on the band.

Step 7: Sew the front and back of the stocking, right sides together.

Step 8: Quick-Fold the hang tab (5" x 2"), using an iron and pin. (see Finishing Chapter)
Sew the two raw edges of the hang tab, right sides together, to the top edge of the band.

Step 7: Quick-Fold the binding strip in half lengthwise.
Sew the binding strip to the top of the stocking, right sides together.
Bring the binding to the inside of the stocking.
Sew a decorative machine stitch, or hand stitch
the binding in place.

Add cording, rick rack and lace trims for an extra special touch to your Christmas stockings.

Other Christmas projects can be found in "Starmakers Ablaze II", "Strip Quilting" and "Strip Quilting Projects 2"

PROJECT 3: RAIL FENCE WALL HANGING or CARDTABLE COVER

Finished size: 36"x36"

Fabric:

floral	1 yard
teal	1/4 yd
mauve	1/4 yd
borders mauve	1/3 yd (if cut across width of fabric)
	1 yd (if side borders are cut lengthwise) see finishing chapter
binding (mauve)	1/3 yd
backing	40"x40"
batting	40"x40"

Step 1: Cut the following strips for the 36 blocks:

floral fabric	7 strips	5" x 44/45"
teal	3 strips	1-1/2" x 44/45"
mauve	4 strips	1-1/2" x 44/45"

Step 2: Sew a 5" wide floral strip to each of the 1-1/2" teal & mauve strips. Press (see accurate pressing instructions).

Cut these combination strips into squares, approximately 6".

Cut 16 pieces

Cut 20 pieces

Step 3: Lay out your design using this diagram.

Step 4: Sew the blocks into rows.
Press the seam allowances of each row in opposite directions.

Step 5: Sew rows together.
Match seam allowances carefully.

ADD BORDERS

Step 1: Measure the two sides of your quilt top, approximately 31".
Cut side borders this exact length x 3" wide.
Fold the border strips in half lengthwise to find the exact center.
Pin the ends and exact center of the border strip to the two ends and exact center of the side.

Step 2: Sew with the border strip on top, right sides together.
Press seam allowances toward the border strips.

Step 3: Measure the top and bottom of your quilt top, approximately 36".
Cut borders this exact measurement.
Pin borders to quilt top, matching ends and exact center.
Sew. Press seam allowances toward the border strips.

FINISH YOUR QUILT

Step 1: Layer it together. (see finishing directions)

Step 2: Quilt it by hand or machine.

Step 3: Add a mitered binding.

More interesting 2-strip designs are in "Quilt Like A Pro" by Kaye Wood

PROJECT 4: PLACEMAT WITH STRIP TRIM
Finished Size: 13" x 18"

4 placemats with napkin pockets

Fabric:

Placemats:
3/4 yd. pre-quilted, double sided fabric

Strips:

Wide strip (blue)	2 strips 3" x 44/45"
Medium (rust) strip	2 strips 1-1/2" x 44/45"
Narrow (tan) strip	2 strips 1" x 44/45"

Pocket - 8 4"x4" squares from two of the strip fabrics.
Pocket lining - 4 4"x4" squares of the third fabric.
Binding - 3" wide x 65" long bias strips for each placemat

Step 1: Cut out 4 placemats 13" x 18" from the pre-quilted fabric.

Step 2: Make the trim:
Quick-Fold these strips in half lengthwise, right side out.(see Finishing Chapter),
the medium (1-1/2") strip
and the narrow (1") strips

Step 3: On the wide (3") strips, press a 1" fold lengthwise, right side out.

Step 4: Layer the folded strips:

narrow tan strip on top,
medium width strip in the middle,
wide blue strip on bottom

keep the raw edges of the folded strips even with the raw edge of the 1" fold of the wide strip.

Stitch close to the raw edges.

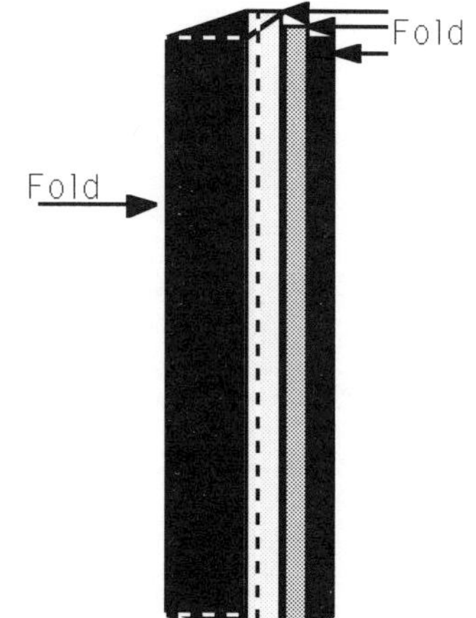

Step 5: Bring the other raw edge of the wide strip to the raw edges of all the strips.

Press.

Fold and pin over all of the the raw edges.

Step 6: Place the layered strips on the placemat, approximately 1-1/2" from the outside edge. Top stitch on the folded edge of the wide strip. through all layers and the placemat

POCKET:

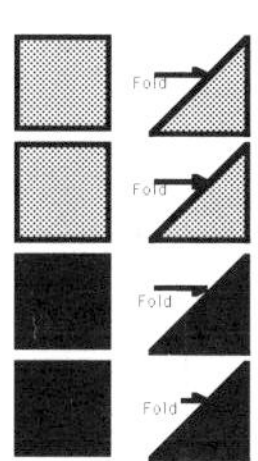

Step 7: Choose two of the fabrics for the pocket; the third fabric becomes the pocket lining.

Fold 2 squares from each of the 2 fabrics (4 squares for each pocket) diagonally into triangles; press

Step 8: Overlap folded edges of triangles; the raw edges form a square. Place the overlapped triangles on top of the pocket lining square.

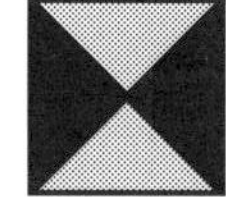

Step 9: Sew all 4 edges of the square. Turn through the middle of the overlapped triangles.

Step 10: Pin pocket on placemat, approximately 2" from bottom and 1-1/2" from side. Be sure to leave "hanky room"; that means-- don't pin the top of the pocket flat against the placemat; move the sides in closer to the center so a napkin will fit in the pocket.

Step 11: Topstitch on 3 sides (leave top open)
Lock stitches 1/2" from top of pocket.
(lower feed dogs or set stitch length on 0)

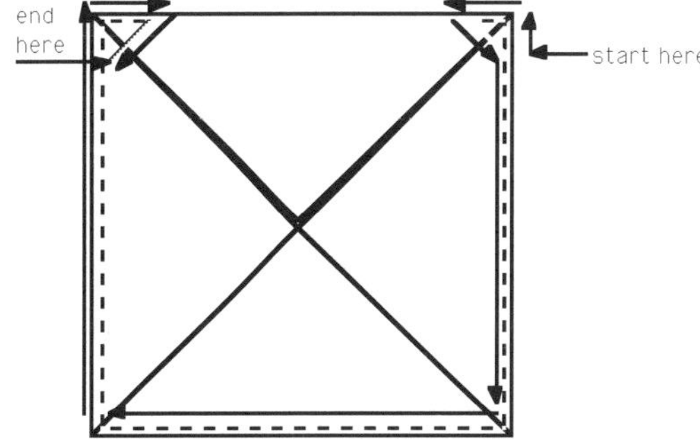

Sew to top of pocket
Pivot needle and sew across top for 1/2"
Pivot needle and sew diagonally back to beginning point
Continue sewing around pocket to top of pocket

Pivot needle and sew across top for 1/2"
Pivot and sew diagonally back to sewing line.
Lock stitches (lower feed dogs & take several stitches in one place).

Step 12: Round the corners of the placemats using the curve of a saucer or small plate.

Step 13: Finish placemats with a double-fold bias binding. (See Finishing Chapter)

Project 5: BISCUIT PILLOW
Finished size: 14"x14"

Supplies:

14" pillow form
fabric (light colored solid) for back of biscuits - one 16" X 16" square

pillow top	2 strips of floral -	4" x 44/45
	2 strips of teal solid	4" x 44/45"
	2 strips of purple solid	4" x 44/45"

fiberfill to stuff biscuits
pillow back 2 15"x20" pieces

Step 1: Sew six 4" strips together into a combination strip:
Cut the combination strips into nine 4" segments (cut combinations)

floral
teal
purple
floral
teal
purple

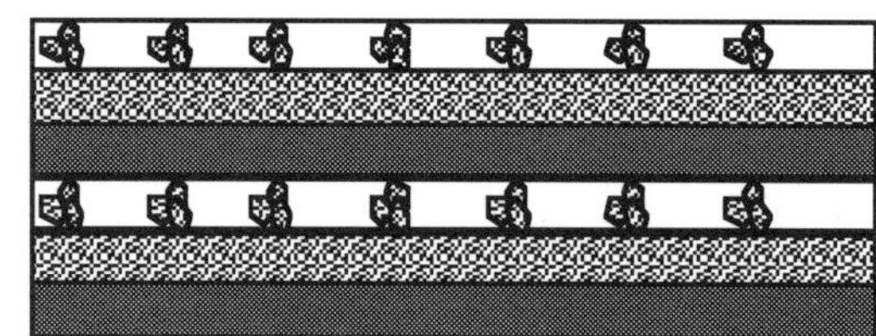

cut 9 segments

Step 2: Sew the 9 cut combinations together lengthwise into one long strip.

Remove the stitches after every 7 squares in this strip.

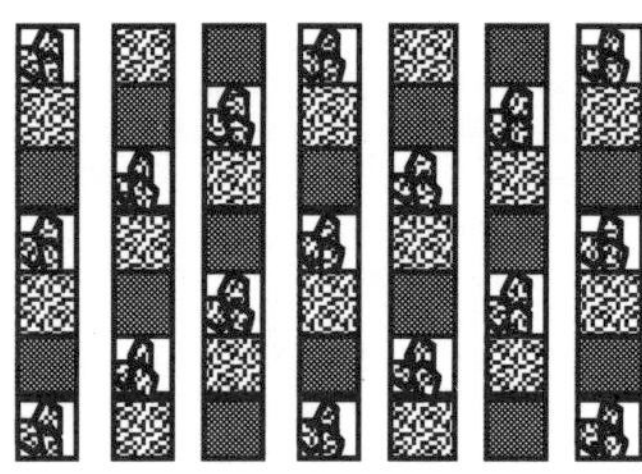

5 squares leftover

You now have 7 rows with 7 squares in each. (There will be 5 squares left over)

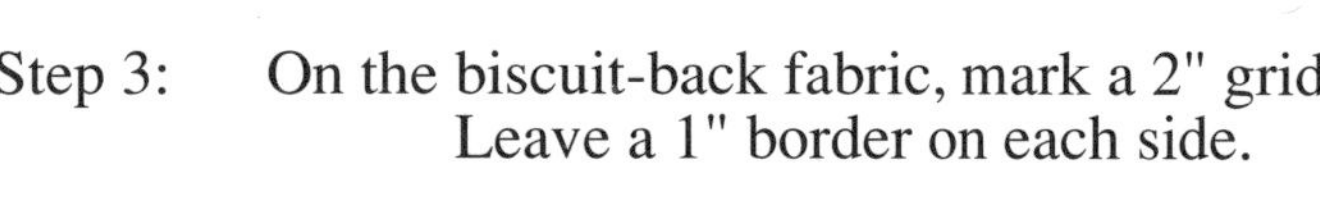

Step 3: On the biscuit-back fabric, mark a 2" grid.
Leave a 1" border on each side.

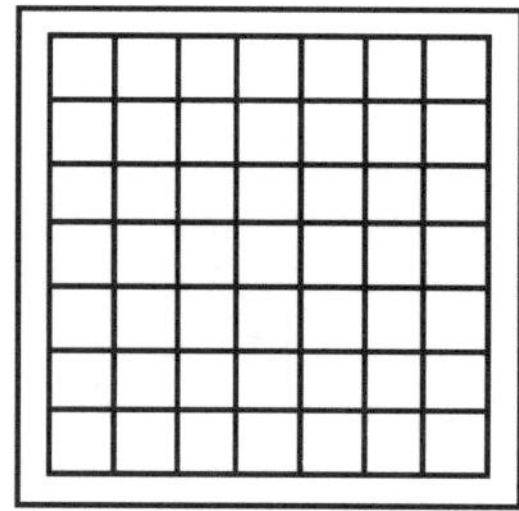

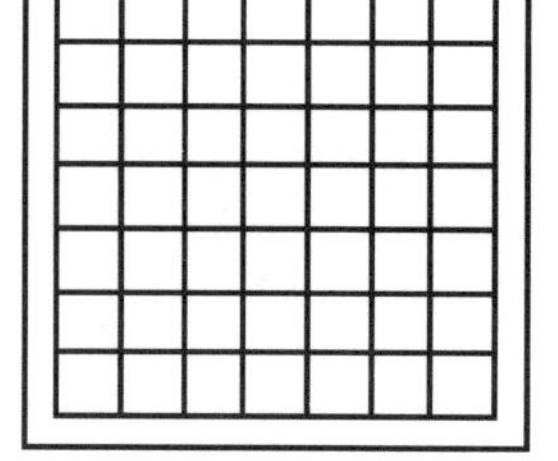

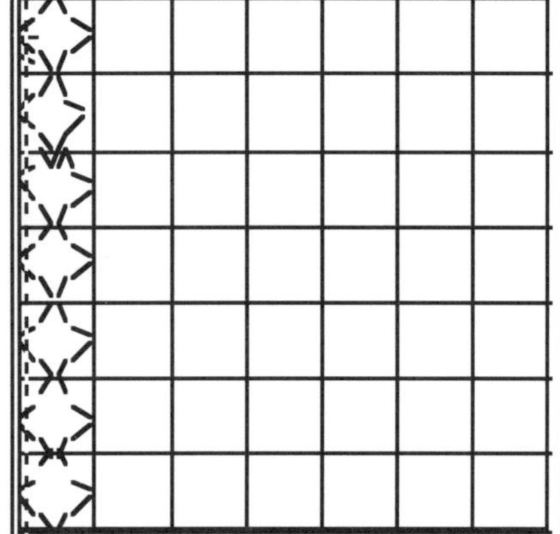

Step 4: Sew the cut combination rows to the fabric marked with 2" grids.

Place the first row, wrong side down, on the left side of the grid.

Pin the seam lines on the left side of the combination strip to the marked lines.

Sew along the far left side, making pleats in each square of the combination strip.

Step 5: Pin the other side of the combination strip to the next line on the grid, matching seam lines to marked lines.
Also place a pin between each square on the combination strip.
This will keep the fiberfil in place.
(These pins will be removed in Step 9).

Step 6: From the open side, stuff the biscuit with fiberfil.

Step 7: Sew the second side of the cut combination strip, pleating each square.

Step 8: Pin the second cut combination strip, right side down, on top of the first combination strip, matching seam lines to drawn lines.
Pleat and sew.

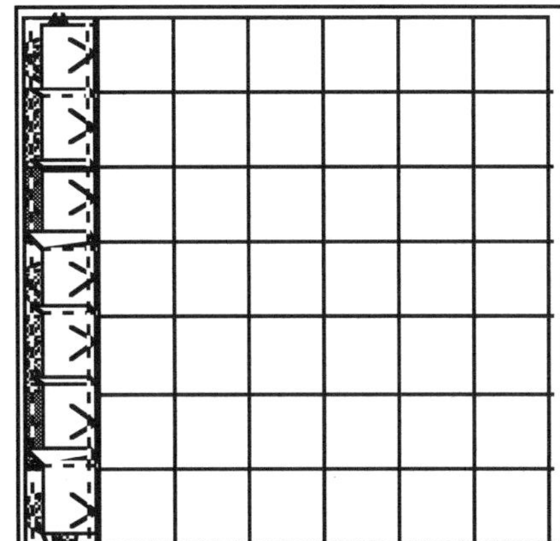

Continue with Step 6 thru 9 until all of the combination strips are sewn to the biscuit backing.

Step 9: Topstitch along the seamline between the squares in the combination strips.
Remove the pins as you sew each section.

PILLOW BACKING

Step 1: Fold each of the 15"x20" pillow back pieces in half, so each measures 15" x 10".
Topstitch 1/2" from each of the folded edges.

Trim off 1/4" from the edges at the fold.
(This will keep the folded edge hugged tight to the pillow, instead of gapping).

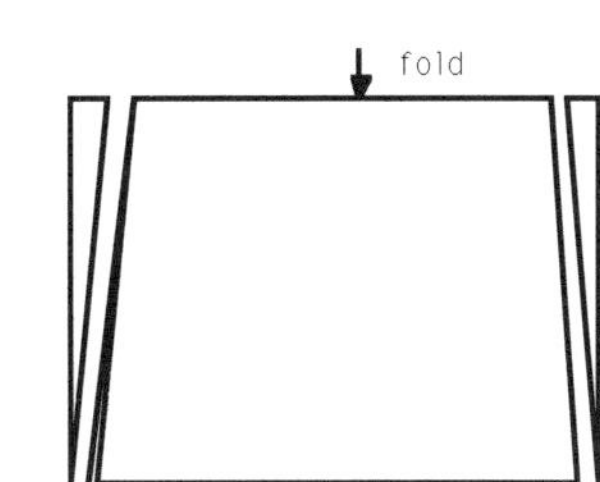

Step 2: Pin the 2 pieces to the biscuit top, right sides together, the raw edges even with the outside edge of biscuit top.
The folded edges will overlap.

Step 3: Sew around all four sides of the pillow, following the stitching line on the pillow top.

Step 4: Turn through folded edges of the pillow backing.

Step 5: Insert the pillow form. If you prefer to stuff your pillow with polyfil, you will have to close up the folded opening by hand.

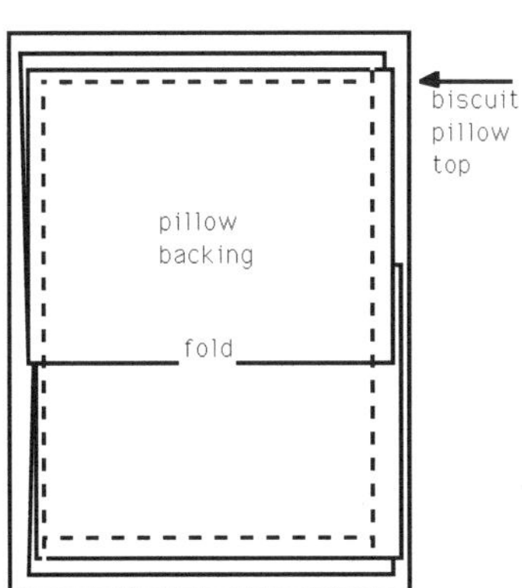

A biscuit basket, using strip piecing methods, is included in "Strip Quilting Projects" by Kaye Wood

PROJECT 6: BARGELLO WALLHANGING

Finished size: 24" x 27"

(This wallhanging is made from the same combination strip as Project 5, the Biscuit Pillow)

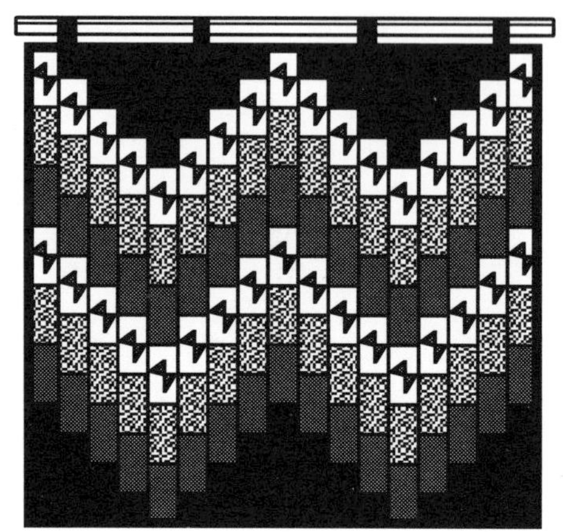

Fabric needed:

Top	floral fabric	1/4 yd
	teal	1/4 yd
	purple	1/4 yd
	black	1/3 yd
Backing	25" x 28"	
Binding & hang tabs	black	1/4 yd
Batting	25" x 28"	

Step 1: Cut the following strips

2 strips floral	4" x 35"
2 strips teal	4" x 35"
2 strips purple	4" x 35"
8 strips black	2" x 10"
3 strips binding & tabs	2" x 44/45"

Step 2: Sew 6 strips together into a combination strip

Step 3: Cut the combination strip into 17 2" wide cut combinations.

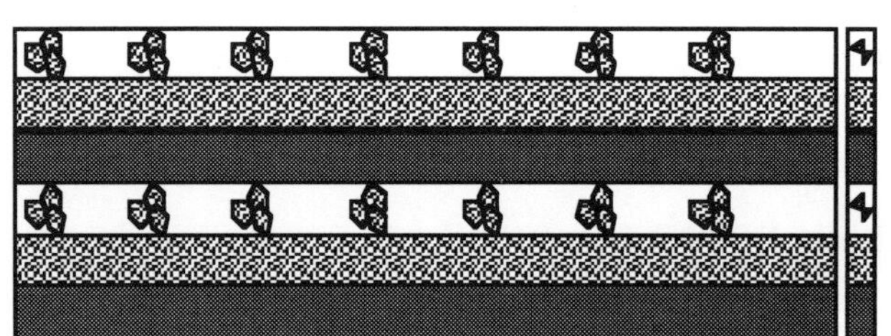

cut 17
segments

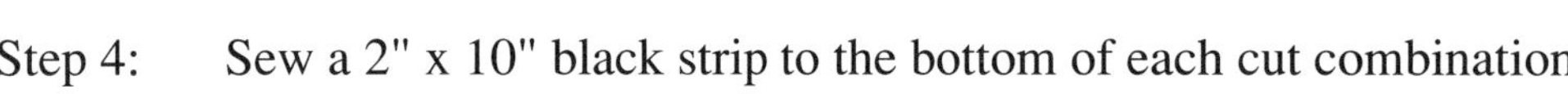

Step 4: Sew a 2" x 10" black strip to the bottom of each cut combination

Step 5: Lay the cut combinations into position.
Drop each piece down 1/2 step.

The black pieces will need to be cut.
Part of each black piece will go at the bottom of the row;
the rest of that same black piece will go at the top of the next row.

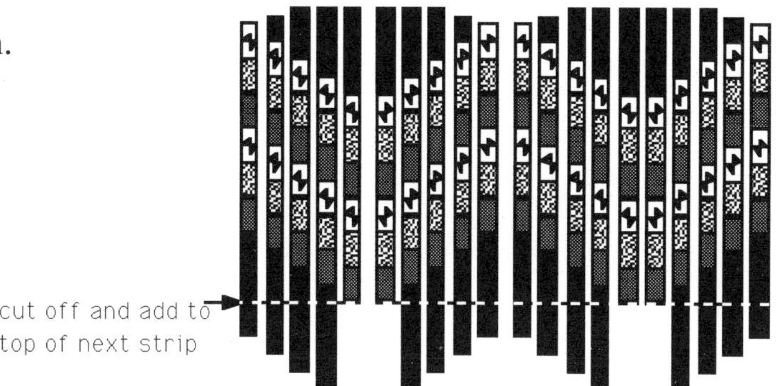

The black pieces will be long enough so you can square up the tops and bottoms when done.

Step 6: Sew the rows together.
Line up the seams in every other row.

Step 7: Trim the top and bottom black strips, if necessary.

Step 8: Layer your quilt (see finishing instructions)

Safety pin baste.
Machine quilt in the ditch
Or hand quilt.

Step 9: Add hang tabs for your wallhanging. (see finishing directions)

Step 10: Add a mitered binding (see finishing directions).

Bargello designs can be found in many needlework books and magazines. Most of them can be converted to strip piecing for quilts. They are just one of the many design possibilities included under the title of Seminole piecing--which is one of the original methods of strip piecing.

PROJECT 7: DECORATED TOWEL
(Just a little bit of fabric can give your bathroom that decorator look)

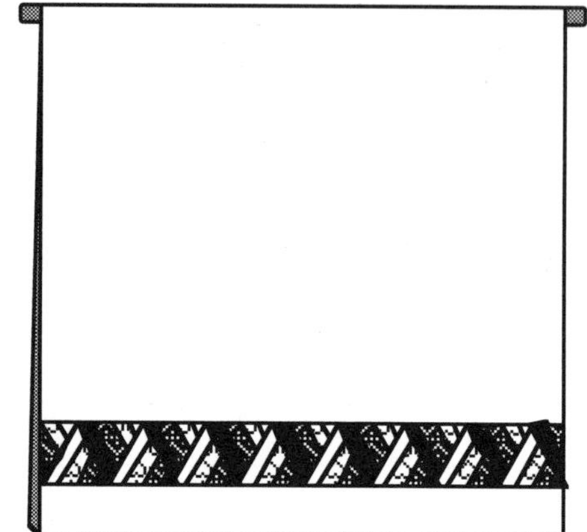

Fabric: Four different fabrics are used--at least one that is dark.

Cut 1 strip of each fabric 1-1/2" x 44/45"

For a 24" wide towel, you will need 13 triangles.
(You should get 17 triangles from one combination strip)

Step 1: Sew the four strips together into one combination strip.
Press the seam allowances all in the same direction.
(see pressing instructions)

Step 2: Use the Starmaker 6 to cut the combination strip into wedge triangles.

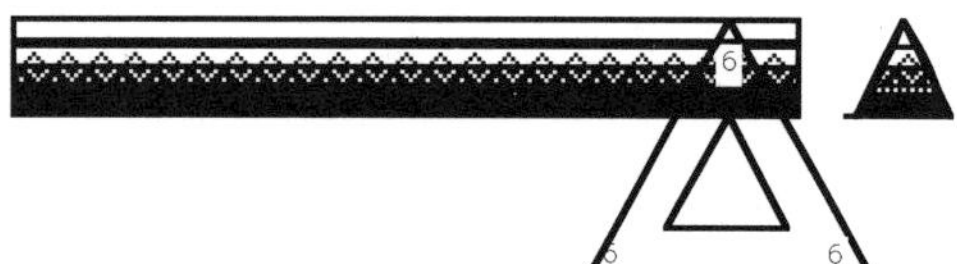

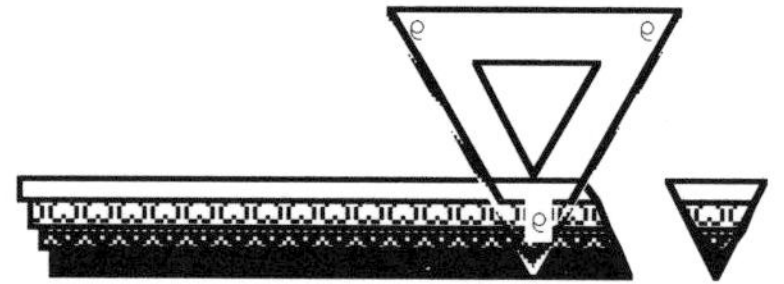

Step 3: Sew the triangles together into a band using this diagram as a guide.

Step 4: Staystitch at 1/4" both long edges of the decorator band.
(Staystitch means to stitch through just one layer of fabric.)

Turn under and press on the staystitching line.
(Staystitching keeps the slightly bias edges from stretching and makes it easier to turn under an exact 1/4".)

Step 5: Cut the band 1" longer than the width of the towel.
Turn under these short edges.

Top stitch all four edges of the decorator band to the towel.

For other wedge-shaped designs, take a look at "Quilt Like A Pro" by Kaye Wood

Project #2
Christmas Stockings

Project #3
Rail Fence

Project #4
Placemat with Strip Trim

Project #5 and #6
Biscuit Pillow and Bargallo Wallhanging

Project #7
Decorated Towel

Projects #8 and #9
Counterpane Baby Quilt and Wallhanging

Project #10
Dresden Placemat

Project #11
Hand Dyed Cosmetic Bag

Project #12
Woven Collar

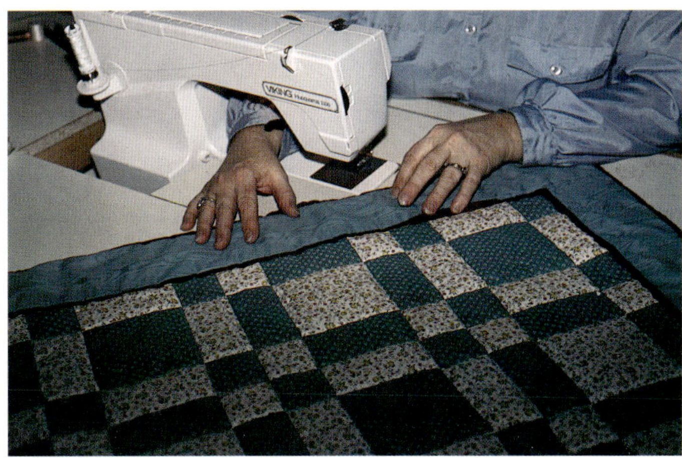

Accent trim on Project #8 is only attached in the seam line.
The folded edge is loose.

Safety pin based to get ready to quilt.

Pinning Diamonds for Accurate Sewing

Insert pin in seam line 1/4" from edge.

Insert pin in seam line of bottom piece 1/4" from edge.

Pin in seam line to follow fabric grain.

Match the ends of the fabric at the 1/4" seam line.

PROJECT 8: COUNTERPANE BABY QUILT
(A 9-patch variation)
Finished size: 40" x 55"

Fabric:

blocks:	dark	1 yd
	light	1 yd
Accent trim		1/4 yd
Borders	dark	1 yd
Backing		1-2/3 yds
Binding		1/2 yd
Batting		42" x 60"

Step 1: Cut strips for blocks
6 strips each color 2-1/2" x 44/45"
3 strips each color 4-1/2" x 44/45"

Step 2: Sew strips together in sets of 3.

Strip A

Strip B

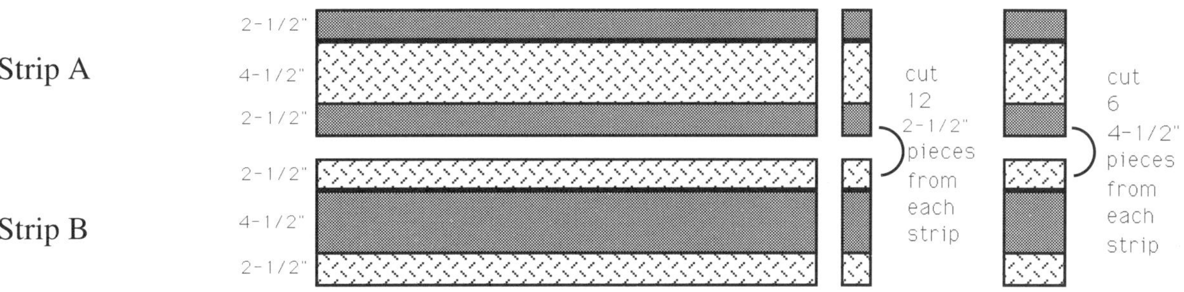

Cut 6 cut combinations 4-1/2" wide from A
Cut 6 cut combinations 4-1/2" wide from B

Cut 12 cut combinations 2-1/2" wide from A
Cut 12 cut combinations 2-1/2" wide from B

Press seam allowances toward the darker fabric.

Step 3: Lay your pieces out in 4 piles

Chain stitch 1 & 2 together
Chain stitch 3 & 4 together

Add 1 to 1&2
Add 3 to 3&4

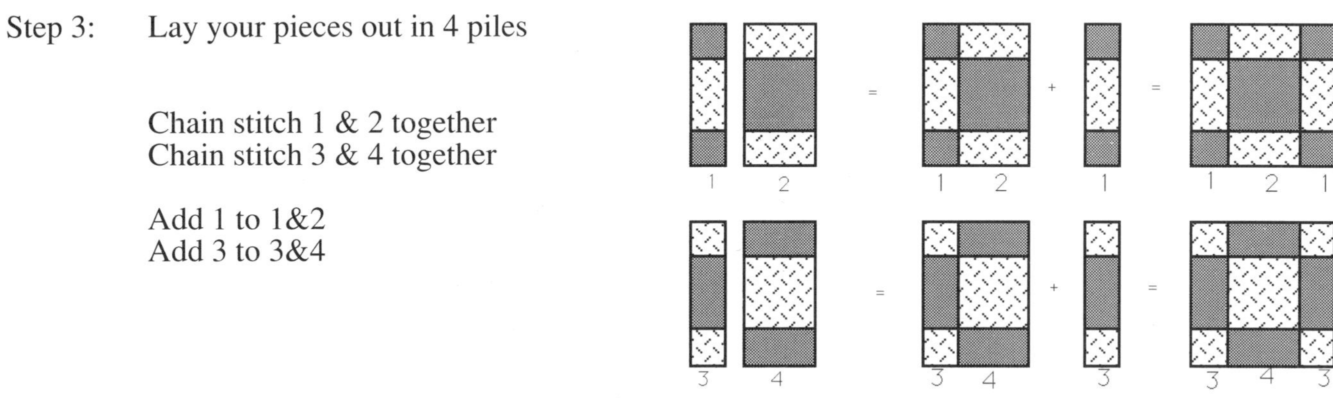

24 blocks are needed-12 of each design

Step 5: Sew blocks into 6 rows.

Press seam allowances of each row in opposite directions.

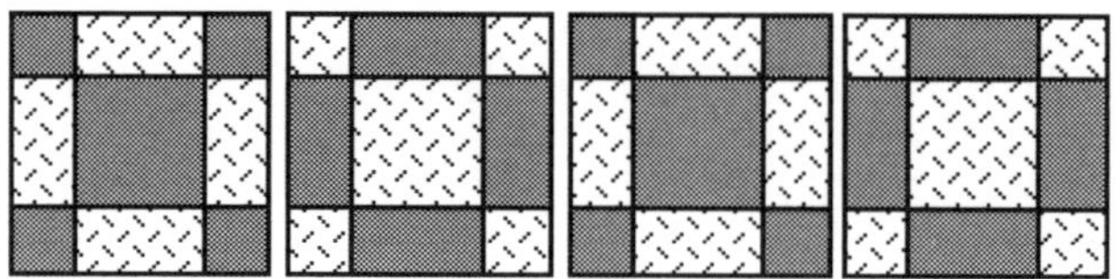

Step 6: Turn every other row upside down
Sew rows together.
Press seam allowances.

Step 7: Accent Band -- cut five 1-1/2" wide strips.
Quick-Fold (with pin and iron) the strips lengthwise.

The accent band stops the colors of the blocks from extending into the borders.
Another form of accent strip might be cording or piping between the blocks and the borders.

Step 8: Sew the accent band to the right side of the quilt top with all raw edges even.
Sew the accent band to the sides of the quilt first, then to the top and bottom.
The accent band is only attached in the seam allowance.
The folded edge is loose.

Step 9: Cut 6 border strips 4" x 44/45"
The two side borders will have to be pieced.
See Finishing Chapter for measuring the length of border strips.

Step 10: Sew the side borders on, right sides together.
Press seam allowances toward the borders.

Step 11: Sew the top and bottom borders on, right sides together.
Press seam allowances toward the borders.

Step 12: Finish your quilt by
Layering
Quilting or Machine Tying
Binding--Cut 5 strips 3" x 44/45".
(This width will give you a 1/2" wide finished binding which will coordinate well with the accent strip.)
The Finishing Chapter will give you more information.

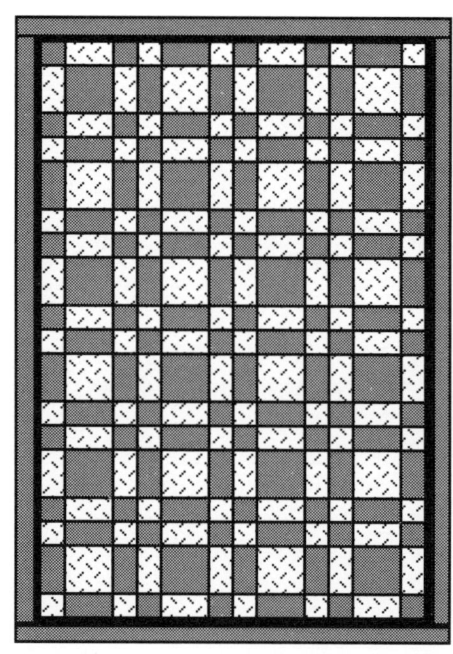

Try the matching Laundry Bag shown in Project 9.

Take a look at Kaye Wood's "Quilt Like A Pro" for over 150 strip piecing ideas.

PROJECT 9: COUNTERPANE LAUNDRY BAG or WALLHANGING
(A 9-patch variation star)

The same combination strips cut for the Uneven 9-patch baby quilt in Project 9 are used here to strip piece a 5-pointed star design to be appliqued onto a matching laundry bag or a wallhanging.

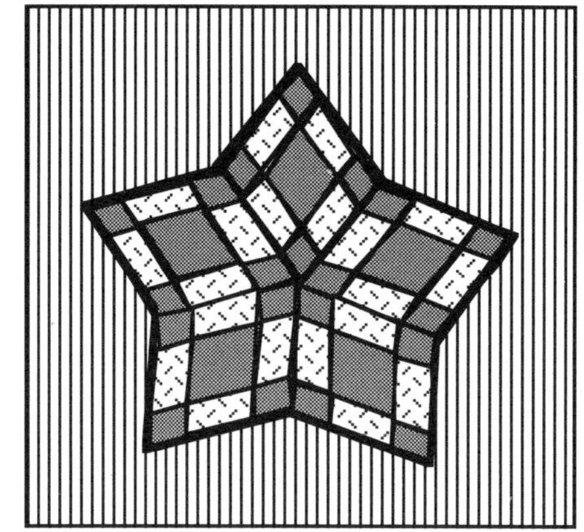

Finished size 27"x27"

An envelope style finish is used.
A casing is added for a rod (for hanging) or for a drawstring.

Fabric needed:

Star	Dark	1/3 yd
	Light	1/3 yd
Front	Dark	1 yd
Backing		1 yd
Accent trim		1/4 yd
Batting		30" x 30"
Binding (optional)		1/4 yd
Ties		1/4 yd

TO MAKE THE STAR:

Step 1: From the dark fabric--
Cut 2 strips 2-1/2" x 44/45"
Cut 1 strip 4-1/2" x 44/45"

From the light fabric--
Cut 1 strip 2-1/2" x 44/45"
Cut 2 strips 4-1/2" x 44/45"

Step 2: Sew the strips together in sets of 3, as shown
Press seam allowances toward the darker fabric.

Step 3: Use the Starmaker 5 to cut the combination strips, as shown.

Place the bottom of the Starmaker 5 on the bottom of the strip at the far left of the strip.
Cut the angle.
On the top strip, cut the combination strip every 2-5/8".
On the bottom strip, cut the combination strip every 4-3/4".

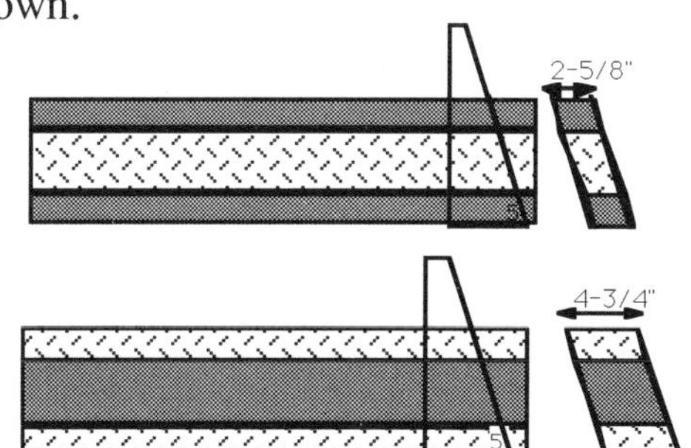

Step 4: Sew the cut combinations into points of the star.
Match seam lines by pinning (see the colored pictures, in the center of this book, which show how to pin diamond points)
Or match seamlines by using the double faced basting tape (see Introduction)

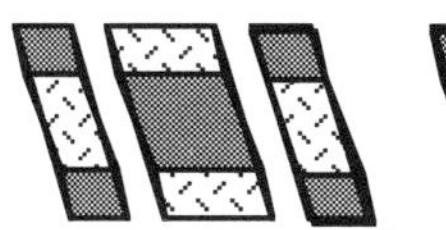
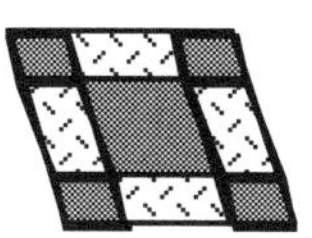

Press seam allowances all in one direction.

ADD THE ACCENT STRIPS

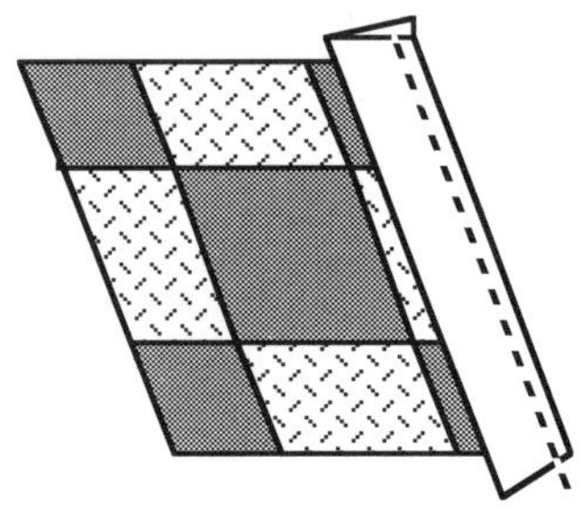

Step 5: Cut accent strips 1-1/2" wide.
This is know as a Hong Kong Finish in dressmaking.

Sew an accent strip to 1 outside edge of each star point.
Sew just a single layer, all the way to the point.

Turn the strip to the wrong side of the star point, pin in place.
Press.
Stitch in the ditch through accent strip and star point.
Trim the point of the accent strip.

Step 6: Sew an accent strip to the 2nd outside edge of each star point.

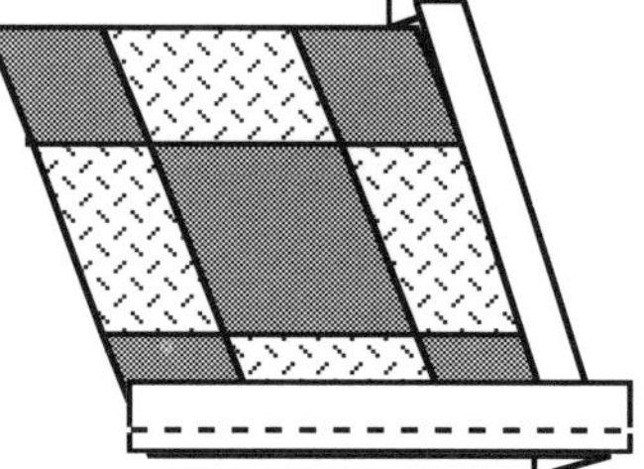

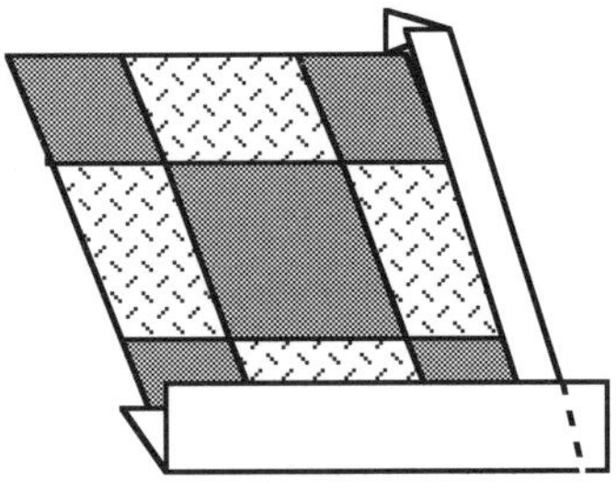

At the outside point of the star, fold this accent strip right sides together.

Shorten your stitch length to about 8 stitches per inch.

Sew the ends of the accent strip about 1/16" outside the angle (to leave turning room).
Trim the ends.

Turn right side out.
Pin the accent strip under the edge of the star point.
Press. Stitch in the Ditch.

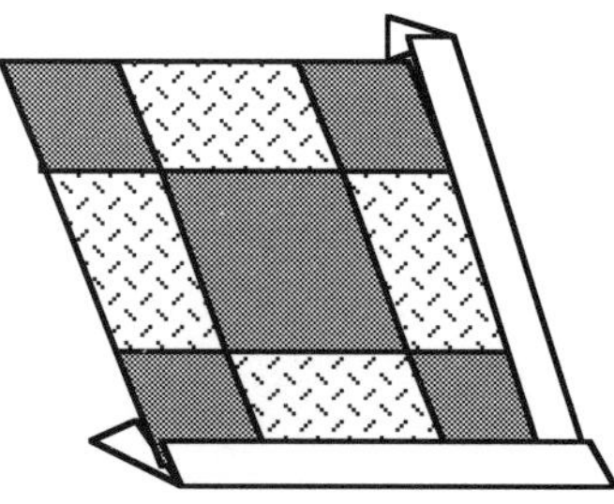

SEW THE POINTS OF THE STAR TOGETHER

Step 7: Sew 2 points together.
Start sewing at center of star, at the very edge of the fabric.
Match seam lines by pinning or by using double-faced basting tape.
Sew all the way to the outside edge of the accent strip.

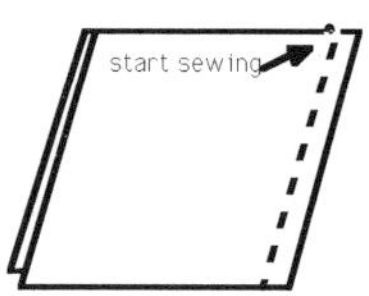

Press seam allowances

Step 8: Sew another 2 points together in the same way.

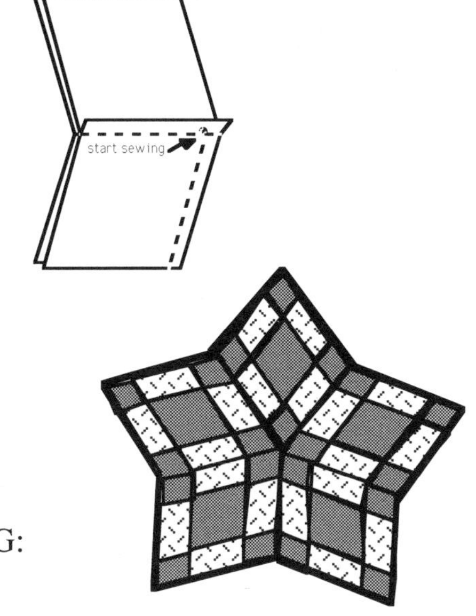

Step 9: Sew these 2 sets of points together.
But, now start sewing at the seamline between the points.
Just put the needle down into the seamline,
Drop your feed dogs (or set stitch length at 0),
and take 3 or 4 stitches to lock the seams.
Sew to the outside edge of the accent strip.
Press this seam allowance.

Step 10: Sew the remaining point--
Match center points.
Lock your stitches and start sewing at the seam line.
Sew all the way to the outside edge of the accent strip.
Press this seam allowance.

TO APPLIQUE THE STAR TO THE TOP OF THE LAUNDRY BAG:

Step 1: Cut the top of the Laundry Bag 33" x 28"
Pin 5-pointed star in place.
Topstitch in ditch through seamline of accent strip and top fabric.

Step 2: Cut backing 33" x 28".

Make a Casing on the front and back:
Stitch at 1/4" from the top edge of the laundry bag.
Fold under and press along this 1/4" stitching line.
Fold under and press again at 2" from the first fold.
Stitch close to the first fold.
Stitch close to the second fold at the top.

Step 3: Sew the front and back, right sides together, on three sides.
Leave the casing edges open.

TIES--Cut two 3"x40" strips of fabric.
Quick-fold these strips lengthwise.
Bring raw edges into the center fold.
Topstitch close to each long edge.

Or if you want to hang your laundry bag up like a wall hanging, put wooden dowels through the casings.

TO APPLIQUE THE STAR FOR A WALLHANGING:

Step 1: Cut the front and back for the Wallhanging 28" x 28"

Step 2: Layer the front, batting, backing.
Safety pin baste together.
Machine quilt through the seamline of the accent piece.
Add some additional quilting or tying so your wallhanging matches the quilt in Project 8..

Step 3: Cut binding strips 3" wide (See Finishing Chapter for more information.

Kaye Wood has many more 5-pointed star designs in
"Quilt Like A Pro", "Serger Patchwork Projects","Strip Quilting Projects",
"Strip Quilting Projects 2" and her video "Starmaker Quilt Designs"

PROJECT 10: DRESDEN PLATE PLACEMAT
Finished size: 15" round

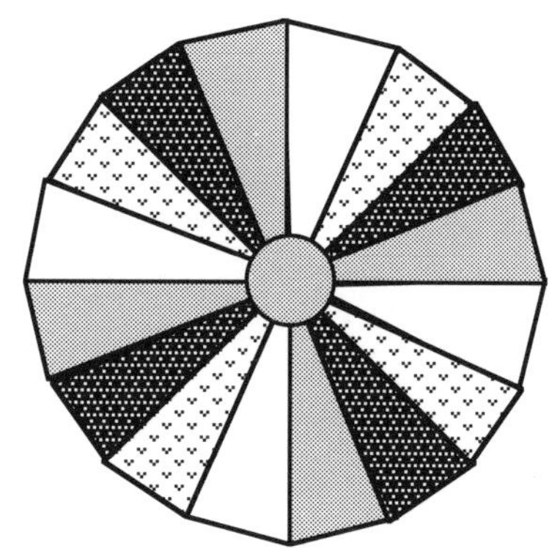

This Dresden Plate design is strip pieced;
It can be done with the sewing machine or serger.
it's so quick and easy, you'll want to make lots of them.

Choose fabrics with different size prints for more interest

Fabric: for 4 placemats

Pieced Fronts		
Four fabrics	1 strip of each	7" x 45"
Backs & center circles		1 yd
Thermore or fleece		1 yd.
Gathered Lace or other trim		6 yds.

Step 1: Cut the strips into wedges for the Dresden Plate
USE THE STARMAKER 8 TO CUT ACCURATE WEDGES.

Step 2: To cut 2 wedges at once, fold the fabric strip in half lengthwise.

Place the line above the "16" on the Starmaker 8 at the top of the fabric strip.

The dotted line on the Starmaker 8 should be on the grain line (at right angles to the top and bottom of the strip).

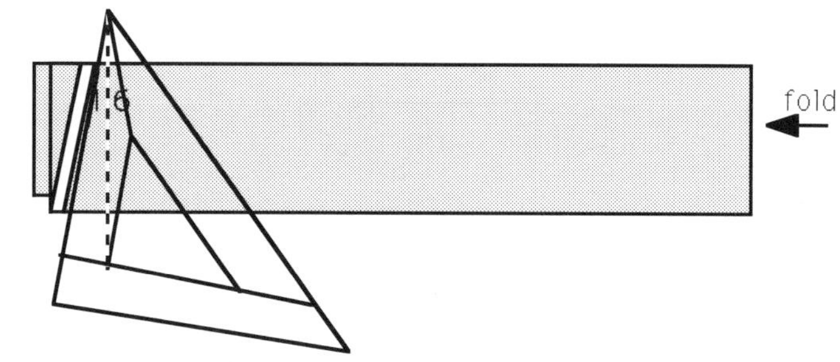

Step 3: Turn the Starmaker 8 wrong side up so the short center line is along the cut edge of the strips.
Cut the other side of this wedge.

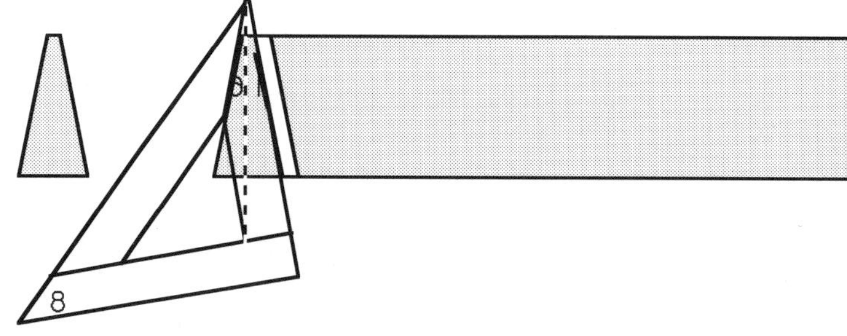

Step 4: To cut the second wedge, turn the Starmaker 8 upside down.

The line below the "16" is now at the bottom of the strip, the short center line at the cut edge.

Cut this 2nd wedge.

Continue turning the Starmaker 8 first upright, then upside down, to cut the wedges.

You need 16 wedges from each color for 4 placemats.

SEW THE WEDGES TOGETHER:

Step 5: Chain sew together the wedges from the 1st fabric and 2nd fabric, in groups of two.

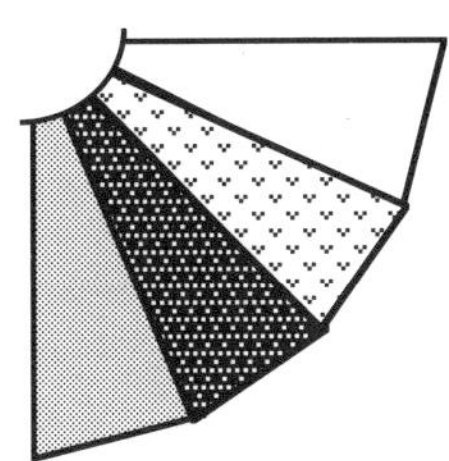

Chain sew the #3 and #4 wedges.
Sew these into groups of four wedges.

Step 6: Sew 4 groups of 4 wedges together into a circle.

Press seam allowances.

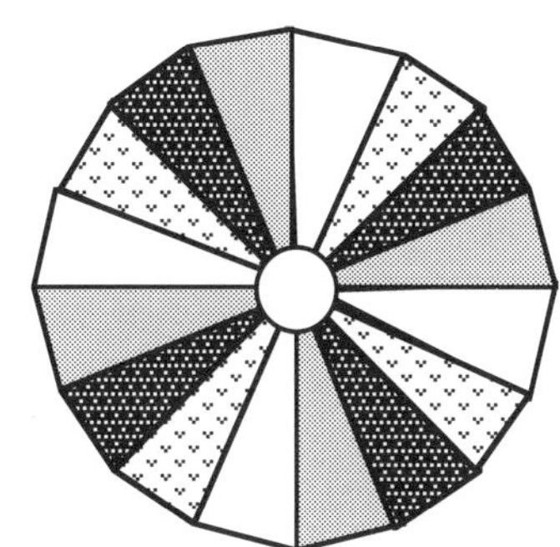

Step 7: Sew gathered lace to the right side of the pieced circles, even with outside edge.

Step 8: Cut 4 backing circles and 4 Thermore or fleece circles using the pieced Dresden Plate as a pattern.

Step 9: Pin together and stitch the outside edge:
the pieced circle on top, right sides down
the backing circle, right sides up
the batting circle underneath

Step 10: Turn the placemat right side out through the center hole.

Step 11: Cut four 2" circles from the backing fabric.

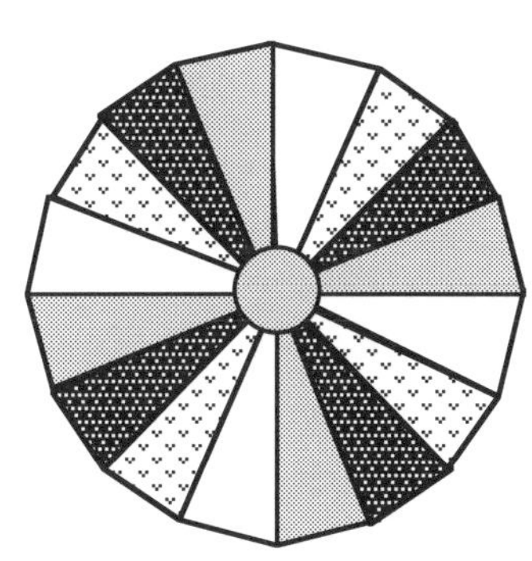

Step 12: Pin these circles over the opening.
Set your machine for a wide satin stitch.
Use a contrast or decorative shiny thread for the needle thread.
Use a back matching thread in the bobbin.
Satin stitch around the circle.

Other Starmaker 8 designs can be found in
"Quilt Like A Pro", "Turn Me Over--I'm Reversible", "Serger Patchwork Projects", "Strip Quilting Projects" and "Strip Quilting Projects 2".

PROJECT 11: HAND-DYED COSMETIC BAG
Finished Size: 6" x 10-1/2"

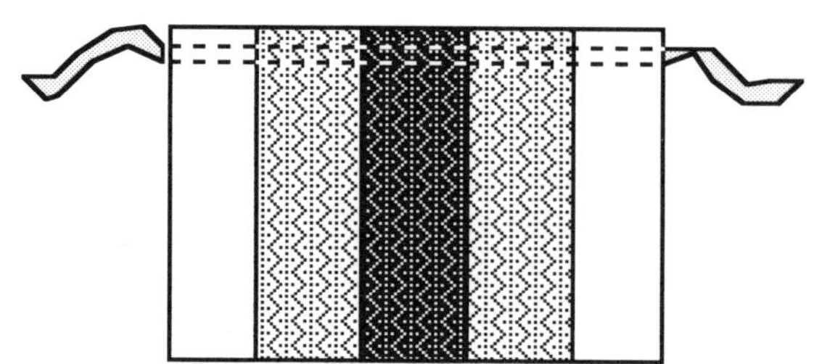

For this project, Marty Lawrence of Flint, Michigan shares with us her hand dyeing knowledge. Just follow her directions--you'll learn how to

use a simple hand spray dyeing technique,
use a strip of lace as our dye stencil, and
combine negative and positive dyed strips,

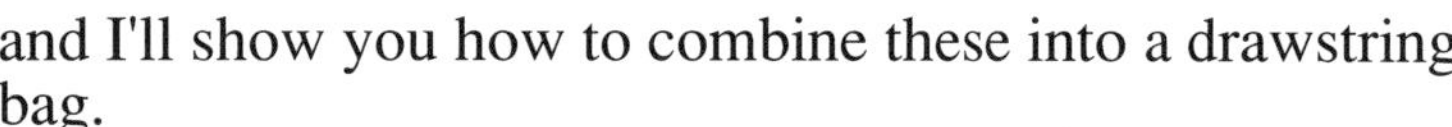

and I'll show you how to combine these into a drawstring bag.

Supplies needed:

1 strip of cotton cluny crocheted lace 2" x 14"
muslin, or other light colored fabric 6" x 14"
lining fabric that coordinates or accents the dye color 11" x 14"
drawstring-coordinating or accent cording.
dye - 8 tsps.
spray bottle
plastic or rubber gloves
urea - 1/4 cup (available from dye suppliers or grain elevators)
Soda Ash - 1/2 cup

Marty used Procion MX dyes because they are the most permanent dyes on cotton.
If you chose to use other dyes for this project--follow the directions provided on the dye container.

CAUTION:Any utensils used by dyeing should not be used for food preparation. Although dyes are considered relatively non-toxic, they are chemicals and should be used with care. Avoid eye contact and wear rubber or plastic gloves. Work in a well ventilated room. Wear a mask when working with the dye in powder form.

The dye solution will keep about a month. Store it in a cool place. Unused dyes may be safely poured down the sink; they will not harm sewers or septic tanks.

Muslin strips, placed under the lace before dyeing, have a negative image of the dyed lace. Two negative strips are sprayed with the dye. These strips (the lace and the two muslins) are then sewn together into a combination strip. A lining fabric is placed under the combination strip--then a small bag is sewn together.

Step 1: Pre-wash the muslin in a heavy duty detergent.

Step 2: Make a solution of 1/2 cup Soda Ash and 1/2 gallon of warm water.
Stir until dissolved.
Soak muslin and lace in this solution for 10 minutes.
Wring out muslin and lace.
DO NOT RINSE
(This solution of 1 cup Soda Ash to every gallon of water can be reused indefinitely.)

Step 3: Mix your dye.
Add 1/4 c urea and 8 tsps. of dye powder to 1 cup of warm water.
(For lighter colors, use from 1 to 7 tsps of dye)
Put the dye in a spray bottle.

Step 4: Stretch the damp muslin fabric flat. Pin or tape it to keep it from moving.
Pin the cotton lace to the muslin.
Spray the dye on the lace.
The muslin will only be dyed through the open spaces on the lace--giving a negative image.
Move the lace to another part of the muslin.

Spray the dye again.

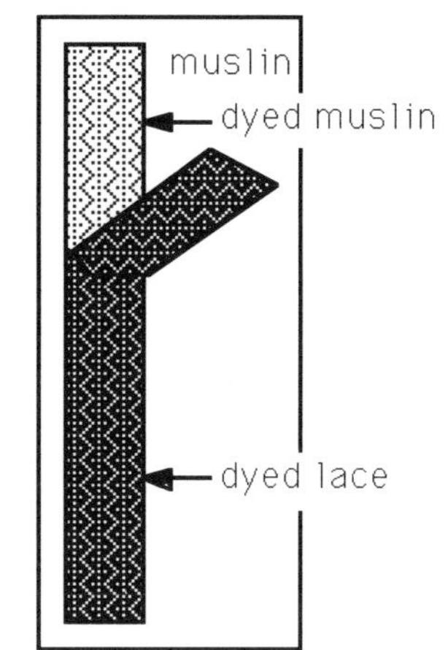

Step 5: Put the muslin and lace in a plastic bag and let set for 24 hours.

Step 6: Rinse in cold water to remove excess dyes.
Then wash in heavy duty detergent

MAKE THE BAG

Step 1: Cut the dyed muslin into strips.

Sew the muslin strips on either side of the dyed lace strips-- lap the lace on top of the muslin.
Topstitch with a zigzag stitch using invisible or matching thread through the lace and muslin.

Step 2: Lay this piece (muslin-lace-muslin) on top of the lining piece.
Turn under the long outside edges of the muslin and topstitch through the lining.

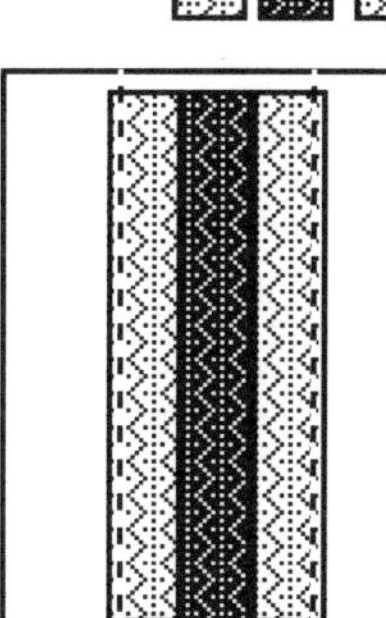

Step 3: Stay stitch 1/4" from top of bag.
Fold and press on this stitching line, toward the inside of the bag.
(Stitching first makes it easier to make an even fold.)

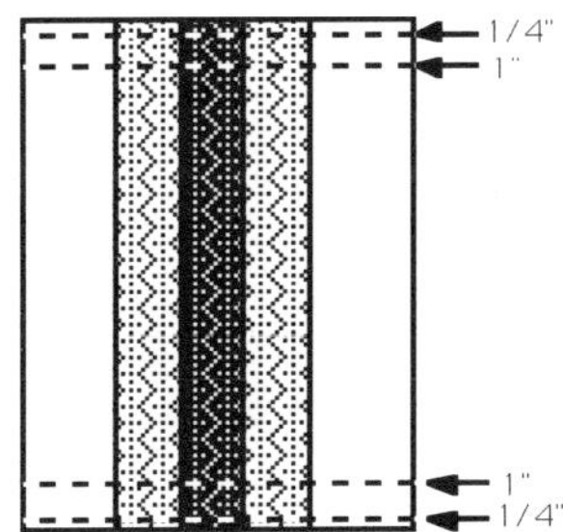

Stitch down this fold about 1/8" from the fold.

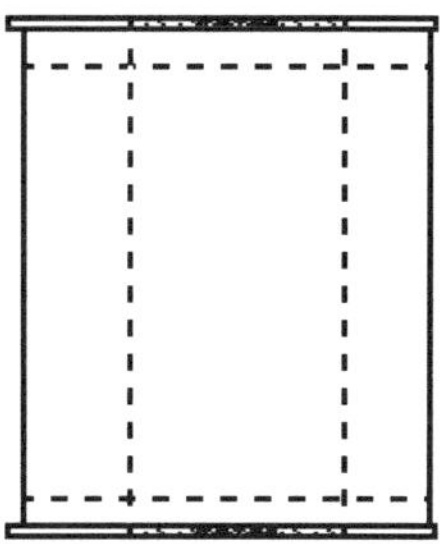

Staystitch a row of stitching 1" from the top of the bag.

Step 4: Fold bag in half, wrong sides together.
This fold will be the bottom of your bag.
Stitch side seams from the fold up to 3/4" below the stitching line 1" from top. Lock threads.
Stitch from 1" line to top of bag.
The side seam from the 1" line down 3/4" will be open for your drawstring.

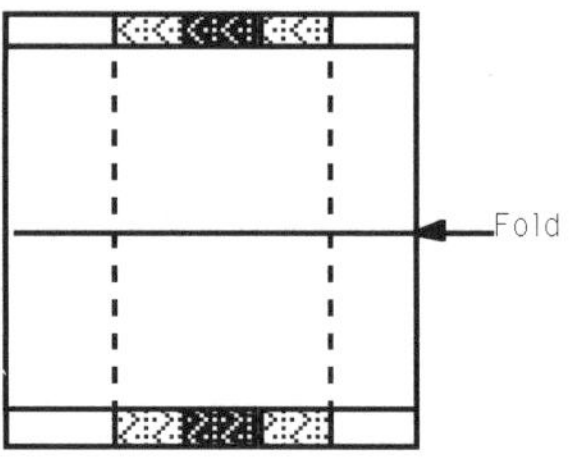

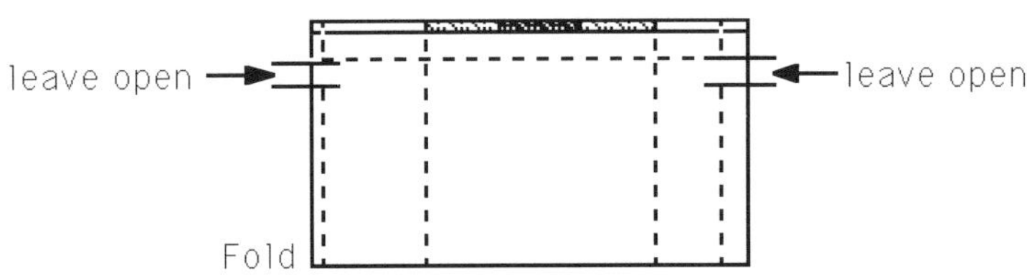

Step 5: Press seam allowances open.
Topstitch through seam allowance and bag around the opening left for the drawstring.

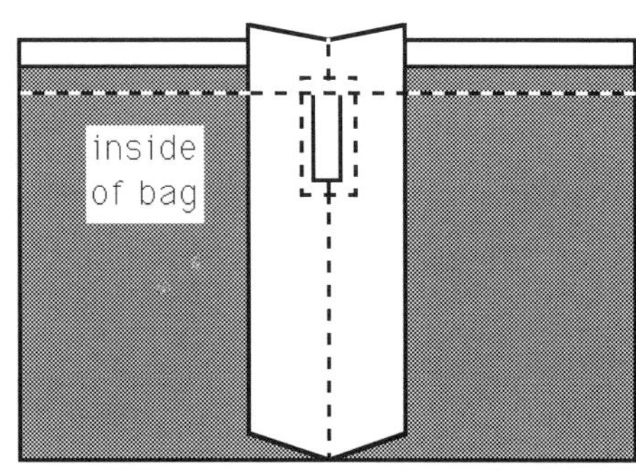

Step 6: Fold down, wrong sides together, on the 1" stitching line.
Press.
Inside, next to the fold, lay the drawstring.
Stitch at the bottom of the casing.

Your bag is finished.

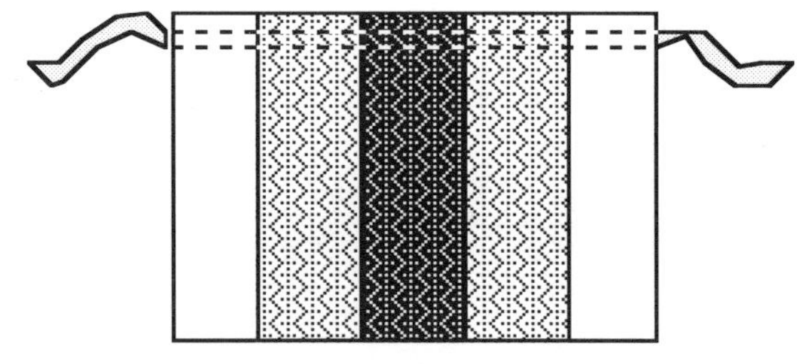

For more information on making, using or buying hand-dyed fabrics, send a legal size self-addressed envelope (LSASE) to:

Marty Lawrence
P.O. Box 4602
Flint, MI 48504

PROJECT 12: WOVEN COLLAR

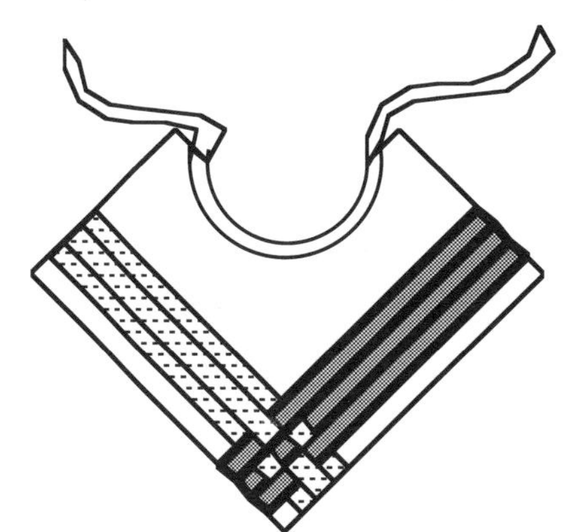

This collar trimmed with woven strips of fabric will dress up your favorite outfit. Or use it to display your favorite quilt pins.

Fabric:

Collar & Facing		1/2 yd
Strips	3 strips dark	2" x 15"
	3 strips medium	2" x 15"
Binding strip		2-1/2" x 35" cut on bias

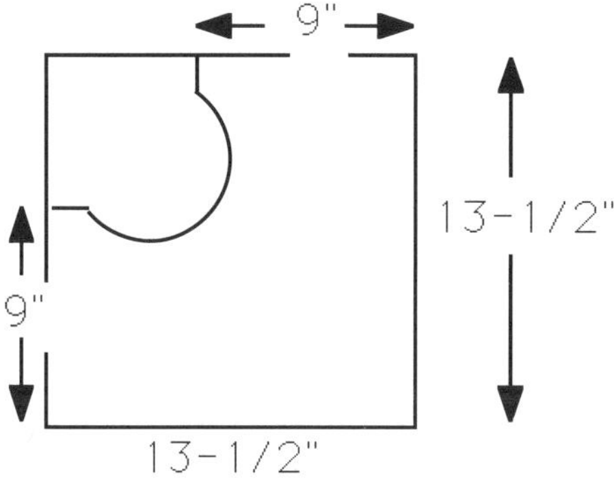

Step 1: Cut the collar and facing using the pattern given.

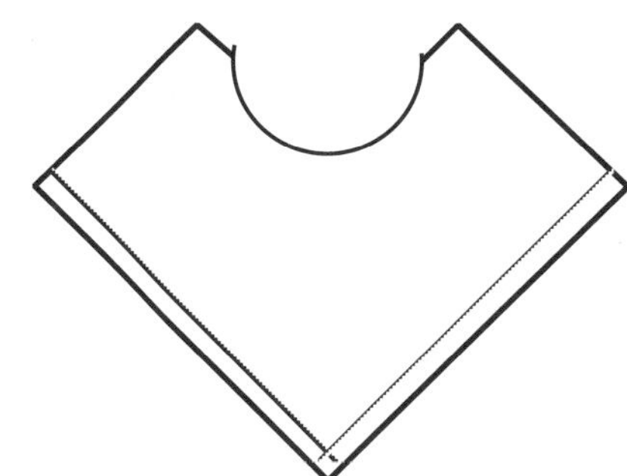

Step 2: On the collar, mark lines 1" from both long edges, using a chalk marker or disappearing ink marker.

Step 3: Cut the strips 2" wide
Quick-Fold the strips in thirds.
Topstitch 1/8" from the long edges of each strip.

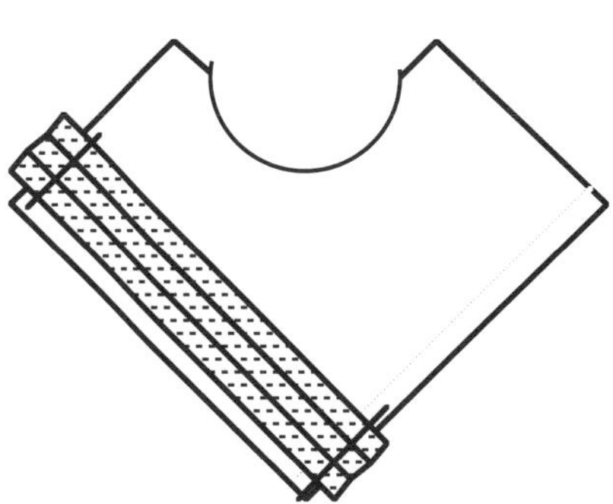

Step 4: Pin the first strip along one of these marked lines.
Pin two more strips right next to this first strip.
Sew both ends of the strips in the seam allowances of the collar.

Step 5: Pin the other three strips on the other long edge, starting at the marked line.

Sew only one end of these strips in the seam allowances of the collar.

Step 6: Weave the strips.
Sew the remaining ends of the 2nd three strips in the seam allowance of the collar.

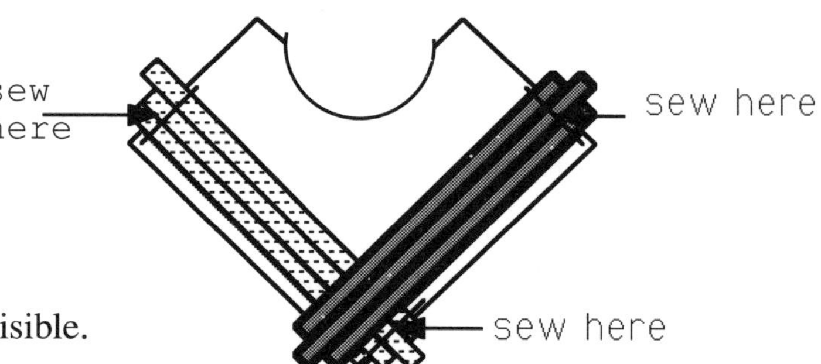

Step 7: Topstitch between the strips just in the woven area.
The topstitching should be almost invisible.

Step 8: Sew two collars (collar & facing), right side together.

Leave the curved neckline open for turning.

Start sewing at the one edge of the neckline; sew around the collar; stop at the other edge of the neckline.

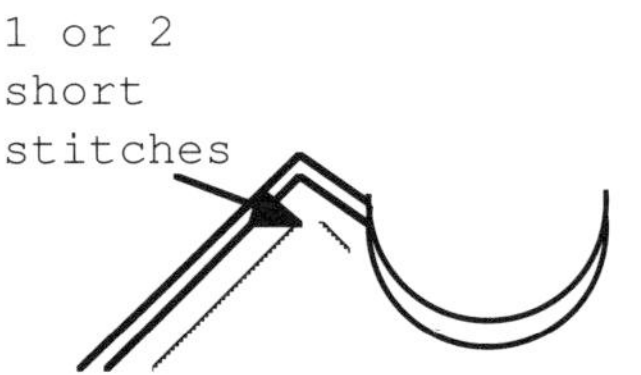

To have really nice square corners,
shorten the stitch length as you get close to each corner.
Take one or two stitches across the corner,
then sew to the next corner.

Press the seam line. Turn right sides out.. Press again.

BIAS BINDING:

Step 9: Machine baste the neckline closed.

Step 10: Cut the bias strip 2"x35" for neckline edging and ties, usingthebias line on a ruler.

Step 11: Quick-Fold the bias strip in half lengthwise.
Pin the center of the bias strip to the center of the right side of the neckline with the raw edges of the bias strip even with edge of the neckline.

Step 12: Sew the bias strip.

Press bias strip.
Trim neckline seam allowance.
DO NOT TRIM BIAS STRIP SEAM ALLOWANCE.

The bias line on the ruler lines up with the edge of the fabric.

Use a rotary cutter to cut on the bias.

Use the lines on the ruler to cut bias strips the desired width.

Bring fold of bias strip to the collar lining.
Pin in place.
Stitch in the ditch through seamline, catching the folded edge on back.

Continue stitching off the collar to the ends of the bias strip.
Press.

CHAPTER 3

PLANNING & FINISHING YOUR QUILT

PLAN YOUR QUILT:

Decide on the size and shape, its intended use.
Gather up your fabrics and sewing tools.

Here are some things that will help you in planning your quilt----

THE DIFFERENT PARTS OF A QUILTED PROJECT:

Main or center part - in a bed quilt, it is centered from the foot of the bed to the tuck under the pillow. This part can be made up of many quilt blocks or one large quilt block. A central design, such as a medallion, should be completely within this area and not extend over the side of a bed. In a wallhanging, the main part is usually surrounded with borders.

Drop - in a bed quilt, the drop is the area from the top of the mattress to the floor on two sides and the foot of the bed. If you don't want the quilt to go all the way to the floor, measure the distance from the mattress to the desired length. The drop can have another row of quilt blocks, partial quilt block patterns, or decorative borders. In some designs, the center part and drop are all made up of the same design.

Borders - The borders on a quilt serve as a frame. Borders also keep the design and colors within the main part from continuing out from the quilt. One or more borders may be added. Borders are also used within the quilt to separate the main part from the drop.

Binding - The binding serves as a narrow border. It also finishes and frames the quilt. A binding may be cut on the straight of grain or on the bias.

QUILT SIZES:

Bed quilts may vary in size according to your wishes. There are "standard" sizes for quilts that may help you in deciding how large your quilt should be:

Crib Quilts - 45" x 60"
Double (Full - 80" x 95"
King - 110" x 105"
Twin - 72" x 90"
Queen - 90" x 105"

A more important measurement is the mattress size:

Crib - 27" x 52"
Full - 54" x 75"
King - 72" x 84"
Twin - 39" x 75"
Queen - 60" x 80"

Make the center of your quilt to fit the mattress size; then add the amount needed for the drop.
That will give you the finished size of your quilt.

FINISHING YOUR QUILT

Now that your quilt top is finished, you have to choose how to finish it and what kind of batting or filler to use. The choice of finishes depends on--

How your quilt will be used - will it be used for a baby and therefore washed a lot. Or will it be a family heirloom or on display to be judged at a quilt show.

How it will be displayed - with hang tabs or a sleeve or will it be used on a bed.

Who it was made for - an eyelet finish is nice for a feminine touch, but a binding might be better for a boy.

BORDERS

Borders are added to quilted items for several different reasons.
They are used to frame your quilt and to visually stop the quilt design from continuing into the borders.
They increase the size of the quilt top. Borders also accent the center design.

Borders should be in scale with the rest of the quilt.
It is better to add several narrow borders than to add just one wide border strip.

It is very easy to stretch borders if you just add strips to the quilt top.
It is much better to measure the edge of your quilt, and cut borders strips to fit exactly.

Borders may be square with the quilt or they may be mitered.

SQUARE BORDERS--

For square borders, cut the border strips to fit the quilt top exactly.
Pin the center and both edges of the quilt top and the border strip.
Sew border strips first to the two sides of the quilt.
Press seam allowances away from quilt and toward the borders.

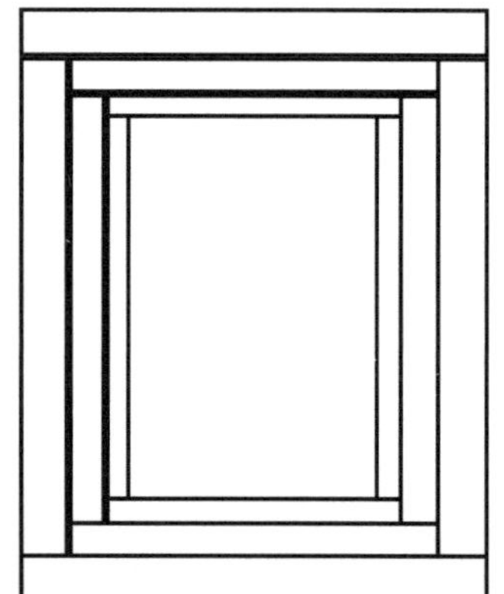

Measure, cut and sew border strips to top and bottom of quilt.
Press seam allowances.

MITERED BORDERS--

Cut each border strip:

5" longer than the length of the side--if the borders are 2" wide.
7" longer than the length of the side--if the borders are 3" wide.

The border strips should extend past the edge of the quilt top and adjoining borders. Begin and end your sewing 1/4" in from the edge of the quilt top. Lock stitches by lowering the feed dogs, or set the stitch length on 0, and take several stitches. 35

Sew all four of the border strips to the quilt top.
(Make sure that all 4 strips are hanging loose at each end.
Press all seam allowances toward the border strips.

Lay the borders in their finished position.
Overlap the extensions.
Trim the border extensions even with each other.

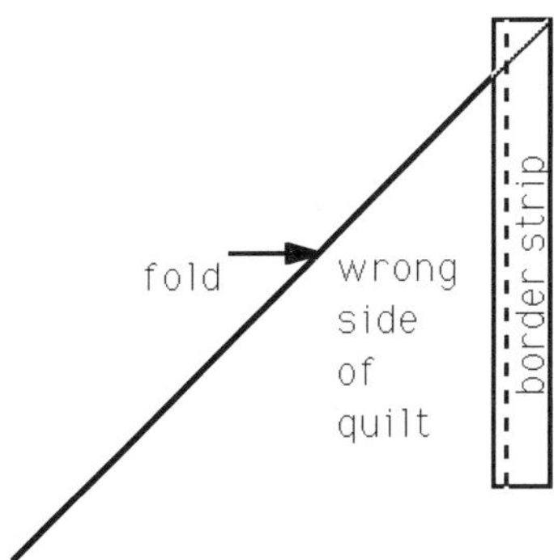

Bring two borders, right sides together.

Sew from the locked stitches on the quilt top out to the corner.

If necessary, mark your sewing line.

Trim the excess seam allowance.

BATTING and FILLINGS:

BONDED BATTING allows us to quilt as close or far apart as we desire, or to even tie a quilt. NON-BONDED BATTING requires quilting stitches to be 1" or 2" apart.

BATTING LOFT:

There are several different weights, or lofts, of batting and each has its own particular purpose:

1. Fleece and Thermore are very thin battings.
   Hobbs' Thermore is easier to hand quilt than Fleece; both are easy to machine quilt.
   Thermore is made especially for quilted clothing because it drapes so nicely.
   Fleece is good for tablecloths and placemats.

2. Low loft battings are used for most quilts or quilted wallhangings.

3. Hi loft battings are especially good for Reversible Quilts, tied quilts and any time you want a quilted item to have a puffy, comforter look.

4. Fiberfil is used for stuffing biscuit or puff quilts and can be used for pillows.

5. Pillowforms are made especially for pillows and will make your pillows look professionally made

BATTING NEEDS TO BREATHE:

Take it out of the package and lay flat for a few hours; or fluff it in dryer.

GRAINLINE IN BATTING:

Batting has a definite grainline. The crosswise grain has more stretch than the lengthwise grain. Therefore, it is important to have the lengthwise grain of the batting laying lengthwise in the quilt. In wall hangings, the stretch of the batting should go across the width of the wall hanging to avoid stretching while hanging.

ENVELOPE FINISH

An envelope, or pillow case finish requires a backing fabric cut the same size as the quilt top. The two pieces are then sewn, right sides together, with or without batting. A binding is usually not used with this type of finish.

Sew around 3 1/2 sides of the quilt; If batting is sewn into the seam line, the batting should be next to the quilt top--this will eliminate the seam allowance showing through from the top of the quilt.

An envelope finish can be combined with piping, lace or eyelet.

SAFETY PIN BASTING.

To baste the layers (backing, batting, top) together, I prefer to use small (about 1") safety pins.
They must be rust proof.
While the backing is still taped to a flat surface, insert but DO NOT CLOSE the safety pins.
(Closing the pins requires you to lift the layers of fabric, so do this after all of the pins are in place.)

Pin 1/2" on both sides of every line that you plan to quilt.
In a large quilt, you might use 400 to 500 safety pins.
Leave the pins in the quilt until you are completely finished quilting.

GETTING READY TO QUILT

LAYER THE QUILT:

To layer a quilt means to stack 3 layers (top, batting, backing) together.

The backing of the quilt should be held taut during layering. This can be done by using a quilt frame or by using masking tape to tape the edges of the backing to a flat surface, such as a hard floor, a ping pong table, etc.

After layering a quilt, hand basting or safety pin basting holds the 3 layers together so quilting can be done without the layers shifting.

The batting, which has had a chance to breathe, is laid on top of the backing. Smooth the batting out, but don't stretch it.

The quilt top is smoothed over the batting. Safety-pin baste, or hand baste, the 3 layers together.

TIE YOUR QUILT BY MACHINE

If you decide to tie your quilt instead of quilting it, you can do it very effectively by machine.

Set your machine for sewing on buttons--a wide zigzag stitch; drop the feed dogs (or set your stitch length at 0). Your thread should match the color of the yarn or ribbon.
Tie the yarn or ribbon; lay it in place; take several zigzag stitches

To just bartack your quilt--set your machine as above; just zigzag without the yarn or ribbon.

MACHINE QUILTING

Bring bobbin thread through to top of quilt. Hold both bobbin and top thread. Start quilting by either dropping feed dogs and taking several stitches or shorten the stitch length to lock your stitches. Use matching thread or invisible (clear or smoke) thread in the needle. The bobbin thread should match the quilt backing. When turning corners, lock stitches to prevent a thread from pulling across the corner.
The stitch length is determined by the loft of the batting--lengthen if necessary. You may need to reduce the pressure on your presser foot.
Don't pull or push quilt through the machine.

STITCH IN DITCH-- Sew on top of the quilt in the seam line between strips.

FREE MOTION QUILTING--Remove your presser foot. If possible, place quilt in a machine embroidery hoop. If a hoop isn't possible, you will need an embroidery foot for your machine. Bring bobbin thread up through quilt. Hold both bobbin and needle thread. Don't turn your work--instead move it side to side, frontwards and backwards.

BINDINGS

A binding finishes off the edges and forms a frame around the quilt. Binding strips may be cut on the straight of grain or on the bias. If the edges of the quilt are straight, I prefer a straight cut binding; it is much easier to handle and takes much less fabric.

How wide should the binding be?
The binding can be very narrow (1/8") to extra wide depending on the look you want on your quilt. If your finished binding (the width showing on the quilt top) is 1/2", then the seam allowance used to join the binding to the quilt must be 1/2" because the binding must be padded with the edge of the quilt. Keep this in mind when planning the width of your last border--your last border will be narrower if you decide on a wider finished binding.

Bindings may be made from a single layer strip, but a double-fold binding will lay smoother and last longer.

To cut a double binding,
cut the strips 6 times the desired finished width of the binding

Finished Binding Width	Cut Your Strips
1/4"	1-1/2"
1/2"	3"
3/4"	4-1/2"

How much binding do you need?
Add 2 x the length of the quilt + 2 x the width of the quilt plus 1 extra foot (just in case).

BIAS OR STRAIGHT BINDING

Bindings may be cut on the straight of grain of the fabric if the sides of the quilt are square. If there are any curves or rounded edges, then a bias binding must be used. A straight binding is easier to apply, but either is acceptable if done well

CUTTING BIAS BINDING STRIPS

Most heavy plastic rulers have bias lines on them.
Line up the bias line on the ruler with the edge of the fabric.
Cut a bias line with the rotary cutter.
For 3" wide bias strips, place the 3" line on the ruler on the edge of the first bias cut.
Continue cutting as many strips as are needed.

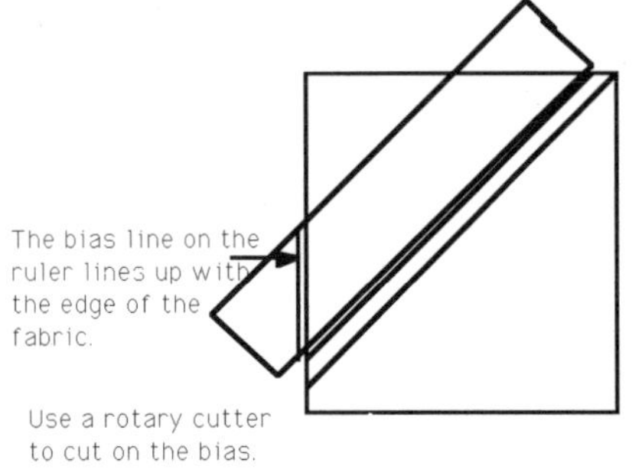

Use the lines on the ruler to cut bias strips the desired width.

QUICK-FOLD

Fold the bias or straight binding in half lengthwise with the wrong sides together, using a long straight pin, an iron, and an ironing board:

> Stick the long pin into the ironing board cover, up over the folded strip, and back into the ironing board. Place an iron to the right of the pin. Pull the strip under the pin and under the iron. It will come out folded and pressed perfectly.

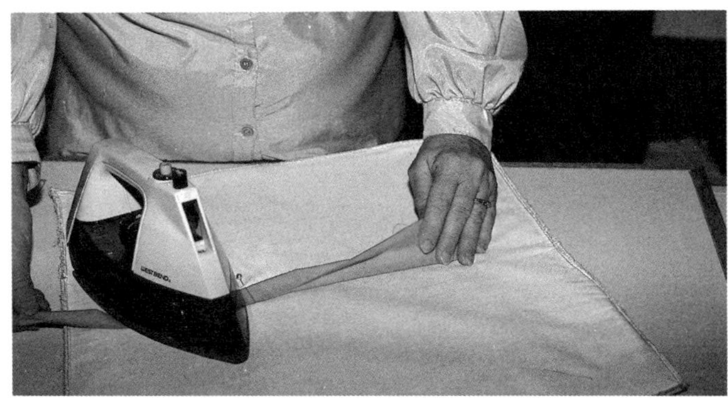

MITERED BINDINGS

Start applying the binding on one side of the quilt--never at the corner. Leave a 6" tail at the beginning of the binding.

Sew with both raw edges of the binding even with the edge of the quilt.

At each corner of the quilt, stitch to a seam allowance width from the next edge.
With the needle in the quilt, pivot the quilt and sew to the corner.
(This will give you a perfect mitered corner on both the front and back of your quilt).

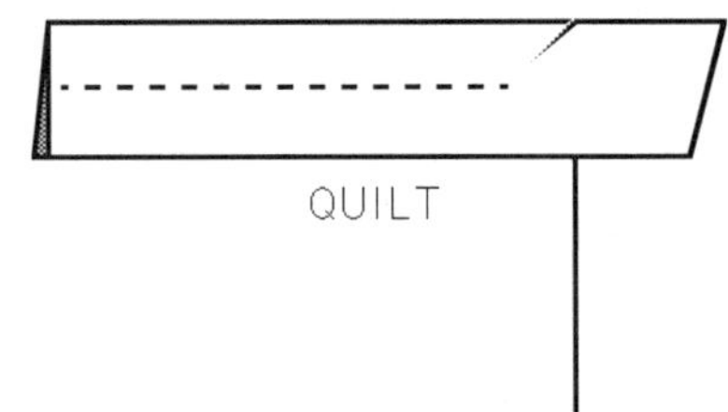

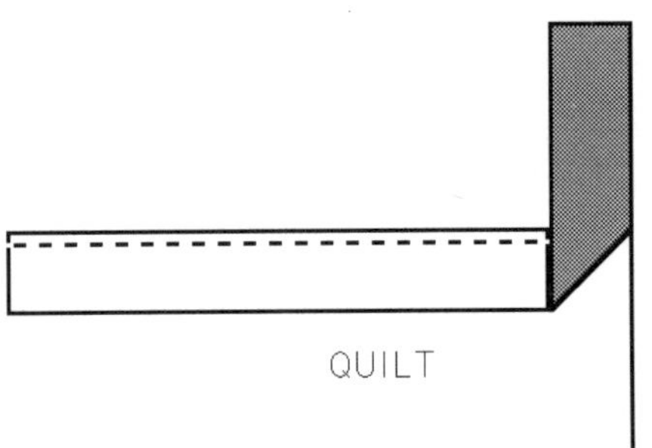

Fold the binding strip up at right angles.

START SEWING AT CORNER

Bring the binding down square with the corner. (This forms a pleat.)

Sew from the edge to the next corner.

Miter each corner the same way.

THREADFUSE™

Threadfuse is a fusible thread that is great for sewing bindings on to quilts. Use the fusible thread in the bobbin; regular thread in the needle. After turning the binding to the back of the quilt, fuse the binding in place so it is easier to sew--and no pins are needed.

FINISH THE BINDING

After turning the 4th corner of the quilt, just lay the binding in place overlapping the beginning 6" tail.
Cut the end of the binding strip so it overlaps the beginning by just 1/2".

Bring the two ends of the binding strip, right sides together and opened up; sew the ends together with 1/4" seam.
This will eliminate the bulky ending that you see on so many bindings.

Pin the folded edge of the binding to the back of the quilt.
OR, if you sew the binding on with ThreadFuse (a fusible thread), press to fuse the binding in place.
Hand stitch; or machine stitch in the ditch from the right side.

HOW TO HANG YOUR QUILT

You can hang your quilt with hang tabs or with a sleeve on the back.

HANG TABS:

Cut a 2" x 20" strip.
Quick-Fold the strip into thirds using iron and pin.
Top stitch close to both long edges.
Cut the tab strip into 4 equal pieces.
Sew the tabs evenly to the back of the quilt along the top edge.
Finish with binding or use an envelope finish.

SLEEVE:

Cut a 5" strip the length of your quilt.
Turn under the short edges and top stitch.
Sew the top of the strip, wrong side of strip to back of quilt, even with top edge.
This edge will be covered with the binding.
Fold under the bottom of the strip and hand stitch in place.

IRONING PAD

On my television show, I use an ironing pad instead of an ironing board. You can make your own pad by layering these fabrics (cut to whatever size you desire, e.g., 24" x 24"):

cotton or sheeting
A layer of fleece or Thermore
a metallic coated fleece, such as an old ironing board cover
A layer of fleece or Thermore
cotton sheeting.

Zigzag (wide, long stitch) or serge all four edges.

SPECIAL OFFERS for YOU

5 QUILTING VIDEOS -- FEATURING KAYE WOOD

KV1 BASIC LOG CABIN
Step-by-step completed quilt
Mitered bindings
Pin basting
Machine quilting
Machine tying
From "Quilt Like A Pro", Chapter 6

KV2 REVERSIBLE QUILTS
Step-by-step
Unique 3-layer quilting
Sewing machine/sergers
Enclosed seams
Reversible vests
From "Turn Me Over--I'm Reversible

KV3 LOG CABIN TRIANGLES
Step-by-step
Easy triangle designs
Precision piecing
Unusual fabrics or "dogs"
From "Starmakers Ablaze I"

KV4 LOG CABIN DIAMONDS
Strip pieced diamonds
Four different sewing methods
Mitered hexagon borders
Precision piecing
Perfect points
Mitered bindings
From "Starmakers Ablaze II"

KV5 STARMAKER QUILT DESIGNS
Strip pieced quilts using the Starmaker tools for precision
Stars, Triangles, Diamonds, Dresden Plate designs
Perfect points
From all the STRIP LIKE A PRO Series books

T.V. SPECIAL---VIDEO TAPES 20% OFF the regular price of $29.95

To order video tapes

1. Send your name, address and phone number

2. We will send VHS tapes unless you specify Beta or European (PAL)

3. Send just $24.00 plus shipping for each video tape*
   Shipping & Handling -- Add 15% (maximum $5.00)
   IN & MI add sales tax
   Payment may be made by check, Visa/MC or COD
      For Visa/MC--
         include card number
         Expiration date
         and the name listed on the card.

*For European System (PAL) tapes only, the regular price is $39.95,
the Special price is $34.00 plus shipping

KAYE WOOD PUBLISHING CO.
4949 Rau Road
West Branch, MI 48661
517-345-3028